You're suddenly alone . . .
and you're afraid!
Don't panic. Follow Lynn Shahan's advice.

1. Don't let yourself be overcome by the enormity of the situation. Remember others have coped and you can too.
2. Recognize that aloneness is only *one* part of your life. Don't regard it as all-consuming.
3. Be aware that a plan you make in a positive frame of mind is more likely to be followed than one you conceive in desperation.
4. Recognize that while you can expect some help from others, you must be ready to do most of the work yourself.
5. Remember that the process of learning to live alone can take a long time.

These steps toward reaching a realistic perspective are only the beginning. Learn how you can become your own person, explore and exercise your options, and find pleasure in your independence, your privacy and solitude.

enjoy
Living Alone & Liking It!

living alone & liking it!*

*a complete guide to living on your own

Lynn Shahan

A Warner Communications Company

The lines from "Gestalt at Sixty" are reprinted from *Collected Poems, 1930–1973*, by May Sarton, with the permission of the publisher, W.W. Norton & Company, Inc. Copyright © 1974 by May Sarton.

WARNER BOOKS EDITION

Published by arrangement with
Stratford Press, Inc., 9606 Santa Monica Blvd.,
Beverly Hills, CA 90210.

Cover design by Gene Light

Warner Books, Inc., 75 Rockefeller Plaza, New York, N.Y. 10019

A Warner Communications Company

Printed in the United States of America

First Printing: June, 1982

10 9 8 7 6 5 4 3 2 1

To my family

Contents

Acknowledgments

I am sure that not many authors enjoy the good fortune of having a sister who happens to be a fine editor. But such was mine and I am deeply indebted to her. To Ellen Shahan—I love you and thank you.

Beyond Ellen's staggering contribution, there are others who were most instrumental in the development and completion of this effort: Gayle Gray, who read draft after draft and made valuable and insightful recommendations; Margaret Weir, who listened and typed and held me together during some rough times; Gary Lewis and Jan Daigle, who were there at the right time with helpful critical analyses; and all of the friends and family members who put up with me through this. Please know that I am grateful.

Foreword

Few people enjoy the idea of being alone. I have seen this in the tear-filled, fear-filled eyes of the newly widowed. I have heard it in the despairing voices of men and women in the throes of separation or divorce. I have experienced it in the frantic efforts of single individuals to ensure busy, peopled lives. I, too, have been there. There and, finally, beyond.

I have come to enjoy being alone, living alone, but not without pain and not without some serious soul searching. It is only after years of thoughtful, responsible solitary living that I have arrived at a place where I can unequivocally advocate living alone as a marvelous lifestyle.

Since living alone is a lifestyle without limits—only those, in fact, which I have chosen to set—it has forced me to live very deliberately, to make decisions very selectively, to ask myself the ultimate question: "What do I really want to do with my time and my life?" I have found the answer in living alone and have realized that if it is there for me, it must be there for others, too.

It is for each of us to discover the joys of living alone—to find that it can be an adventure with its own intrinsic delights. It is for each of us to experience the pleasures that can come from knowing we are capable of living full, productive lives on our own. As I have—so, I would hope, will you.

living alone & liking it!*

*a complete guide to living on your own

1

Declaration of Independents

You needn't be a student of sociology to have noticed that America is in the midst of a social evolution, if not a revolution, in traditional lifestyles: A rapidly increasing segment of the population is living alone.

Once representing a small portion of American homes, single-person households have more than doubled since 1960 to fifteen million. Between 1970 and 1975 the number of people living alone increased by almost forty per cent.

In August 1977 the U.S. Census Bureau disclosed that nearly twenty-one per cent of all U.S. homes—over one-fifth—were inhabited by one person. These inhabitants cut across a wide age spectrum—from eighteen to eighty—which includes young adults, senior citizens, "empty nesters" and others. They represent the unmarried, the widowed, as well as the divorced and separated.

Real-estate brokers across the country report that growing numbers of single people are buying their own homes. A decade ago single people rarely bought houses; now twenty per cent of all homebuyers are single. This trend is being reflected in the housing industry in a new emphasis on single-person dwellings. Townhouses and apartments are now designed with the single resident in mind.

The marketing industry is also responding to the impact on purchasing of the rising numbers of single adults. Goods are now conceived, produced and mass-marketed specifically for the single consumer.

Legislative bodies across the country have reacted by enacting special laws for the benefit and protection of the single person—laws which have made it easier for him to procure a mortgage loan (the single adult was once considered a poor risk); laws which have reduced the discrimination against single wage-earners of federal and state income-tax regulations; laws which uphold the right of the single consumer to buy in small quantities in lieu of bulk-bagged or prepackaged items.

Why this seemingly sudden attention to a once insignificant group?

When you consider that there are twelve million widows and widowers in America today, that one marriage in three ends in divorce, and, according to statistics, that unmarried people will soon outnumber marrieds in this country, it is no wonder that the single person has become a target of interest.

With the increasing isolation of urban American society and the growing fragmentation of multi-generation families, living alone is a very real possibility for many people. It is a possibility which conceivably could confront anyone at some point during his or her lifetime.

BUT I DON'T WANT TO LIVE ALONE!

Except for those who choose it as a lifestyle, few people consider that living alone can be a positive experience. Many people object strenuously to any mention of living alone as a potential circumstantial necessity, even in the remote future. They refuse to believe that a person alone can build a balanced and happy life for himself. Some even admit to remaining in relationships that are unproductive and unfulfilling only because they cannot conceive that living alone can be anything but a dreary, negative existence.

And there was a time in my own life when I would whole-heartedly have concurred.

I Find Myself Alone

For me, living alone began many years ago as a very personal, and not very hopeful, adventure. I had never planned on living alone, so when circumstance thrust it upon me, I found myself filled with anxiety and fear. In fact, I was so desperate that I considered advertising in a local newspaper for a warm body to share space with.

Up to that point in my life I had always lived with other people—first with family, and then with some friends I'd made in college. Never in my worst dreams had I imagined that I might someday have to face life alone, even temporarily. But there I was. And having considered the complications a "want-ad" roommate might bring, I decided to go ahead and face my destiny, though I did so with a great deal of trepidation.

Some reassuring friends helped me locate an apartment, moved me in, then gave me a pat on the back and told me that everything was going to be all right.

"Are you kidding?" I wanted to scream. "I'm all *alone*!"

As I sat in my living room that afternoon, tears in my eyes, a lump in my throat, and a sick, empty feeling in the pit of my stomach, I tried to come to grips with my situation. After what seemed like hours of mental and emotional turmoil, it occurred to me that it might help if I could isolate my fears and deal with them one at a time.

As inconsequential as it may seem, the thing I dreaded most was spending the night alone. All sorts of frightful imaginings centered on this first-time experience. I toyed with the idea of staying up all night; I also considered leaving all the lights and the TV set on and trying to sleep through it. But when bedtime arrived around midnight that night, I forced myself to get ready, put myself reluctantly in the hands of fate, and crawled between the covers.

I fell asleep much sooner than I had expected. In fact, the next thing I knew my eyes were open, the sun was streaming through my windows, and I was pinching myself in disbelief. I greeted that day with a feeling of great accomplishment. I'd made it over the first hurdle!

With renewed strength and confidence I tackled the next fear, and the next, and the next, until I found myself some months later successfully on my way.

Climbing a Mountain

It's no secret that many people live alone without liking it. When time and circumstance converge upon them, leaving them unexpectedly on their own, the necessity to adjust to an unchosen lifestyle is forced as unfeelingly upon them as it was upon me. Most have never before functioned as totally independent adults; these people, through no fault of their own, do not know *how* to think, feel and act as single people.

What it amounts to is that very few of us have been trained in the art of being alone; it is not surprising that we fear the unfamiliarity and apparent isolation of single living. This does not mean, however, that we are incapable of coming to terms with ourselves as single people or that we are incapable of recognizing in time that living alone need not mean living lonely.

As someone who had a rough time adapting to life on her own observed, "Learning to live alone is like climbing a mountain. Once you reach the top, the view is great!"

Is it really possible to live alone and like it?

Yes! I've been living alone and liking it for fifteen years, and I'm not the only one. An overwhelming majority of the people I interviewed on the subject like it, too. Granted, there are some real problems to be faced, some "mountains to climb." For those who must adapt to living by themselves against their wishes, this is especially true. But as I have come to relish my freedom and independence, so, I believe, will you.

If you are inclined to reject the idea of solitary living out of hand, I ask that you keep this thought in mind: *Living alone may be different for you, but that doesn't mean that it can't be essentially good.* This realization marked the beginning of my finding my own way in the world.

WHY WOULD ANYONE CHOOSE TO LIVE ALONE?

In a society where social emphasis is placed on pairing as the accepted norm, no young child planning for his future is likely to say, "When I grow up I want to live alone!" Certainly not in the same way that he might say, "When I grow up I want to be a fireman!"

If a person exists who actively planned during his formative years to live alone for the rest of his life, I have yet to meet him. Living alone, more often than not, is something that happens during the course of one's life as a result of circumstance. It is only recently that it has become an attractive option, as opposed to the dreaded consequence it once was. It *has* become something people *choose* to do. What is behind this trend?

Most of us, when we reached our late teens, looked forward to the day when we could occupy places of our own, away from the confines of our families. This "moving away" was seen as a chance to strike out on our own, to grow, to spread our wings and test our independence. At the same time, we tended to regard this condition as temporary—the "thing to do" until we found our mates and married.

While this attitude and traditional sequence have continued over the years, a group of individuals has emerged to challenge the concept that together is better than alone. Society has felt the impact.

A New Look at the Loner

At one time in the not-too-distant past, the person who lived by himself—the "loner"—was viewed by the rest of the community as weird, strange, hermitlike, even deviant. Since no one in his right mind (or so it was thought) would choose to live alone, it was assumed that such a person was simply undesirable. Until recently, the only time that living alone was deemed appropriate or respectable as a way of life was during the period of transition between leaving home and marrying.

Culturally, being alone has, in the past, had far-reaching social implications and consequences. Society has long attached a stigma to being alone. Not living true to the fairy tale of finding your Prince or Princess Charming was seen in some quarters as sheer defectiveness: *There must be something wrong with you.*

If being married or having a love interest equaled success, then by such a standard being alone equaled failure. The implicit accusation stung upon impact: *You are not capable of attracting and/or holding a mate.* By the standards that then prevailed, it was far better to choose to have someone around and be labeled "successful" than to be alone and be branded a "failure."

It was also assumed that the person alone must, by definition, be lonely, so such a person easily became an object of pity and sympathy. If we noticed someone eating alone in a restaurant, we instinctively catalogued that person as a "poor, solitary soul"; we felt sorry for him. It was difficult for us to imagine that a person might be content in his or her own company.

Until recently we had a tendency to place people without mates into some sort of exile. Today, however, attitudes toward the loner are much more liberal. Men and women who live alone are no longer pressured into defensive positions. They are no longer retreating into gloomy half-lives. Loners are moving out and up in the world and are creating viable niches for themselves.

Singlehood has achieved a new status

and respectability in the last decade, if for no other reason than because it has become a category populated by vast numbers of people. A natural repercussion of this social development is that living alone has acquired a new legitimacy, too. It is now accepted socially as an alternative lifestyle—one that is both natural and complete, one with its own set of customs. In fact, being single has become almost fashionable.

The single life has come to be appreciated as a chance to take charge of your life, to hold onto your options, to live virtually unfettered. The people who have settled on living alone as a preferred lifestyle—whether temporarily or permanently—tout the advantages and praise the opportunities it gives them. Inherent in the lifestyle are the opportunities to:

ENJOY YOUR FREEDOM

In living alone you are endowed with a most significant kind of freedom: the freedom to manage your time and your life in any way you choose. The implications are fantastic!

You are blessed with a freedom others may never know: freedom to explore yourself and the life you are living; freedom to explore the world you inhabit; freedom which, if exercised, can make living alone a less restrictive sort of existence than may be afforded in other lifestyles.

In living alone you also have more leisure time: time to travel, to develop talents and skills, to pursue interests, to find new hobbies, to relax, to meet new people, to entertain and be entertained, to spend your time in any way you wish.

Living alone means having total freedom to make your own decisions—to be able to choose freely what to do with your days, your nights, your weekends, and ultimately your life: To be or not to be, to do or not to do, to respond or not to respond *on your own terms*, to set goals and work toward them, to commit yourself to new ideals on an ongoing basis.

You can come and go as you please without having to account for the time spent. You are free to accommodate the particularity of your own tastes: to do anything or nothing, to try new things, new places, new ways of life. You eat when you choose, go where you want to, come home when you want to, save your money or spend it. You can exercise a certain amount of whimsy in the way you approach day-to-day living. You can be a true free spirit.

BECOME YOUR OWN PERSON

Living alone offers you an unparalleled opportunity for developing a solid personal identity. Indeed, in no other lifestyle are you as likely to discover your own individuality. Experiencing solitary living gives you a chance to know yourself intimately; a chance to draw upon untouched personal capacities; a chance to find out who you are and what your strengths are.

You go out and interact with the world and come home to reflect on it. Because you have so much time for uninterrupted introspection, it becomes possible for you to see yourself clearly in relation to your life.

There are people who never have the chance in their busy, peopled lives to meditate, to ponder their mistakes, or to examine the direction their lives are taking. Stagnation sets in and personal growth is stunted. In contrast, the person who lives alone can capitalize on an optimum opportunity for self-awareness.

In living alone you are left with yourself. You have time for a self-identity search which can be done at leisure and at no one's expense. Periods of total aloneness have a way of forcing you into yourself. This can be an invigorating experience—an opportunity to be "reborn" as your own person. You have more time to think about yourself and your life, and from new thoughts and new insights can emerge a strong sense of self.

EXPLORE (AND EXERCISE) YOUR OPTIONS

One of the nicest things about living alone is that you have ample time for exploration—time to find out just what your options are. The quiet space that surrounds you can allow for the illumination of perspectives you may never have the chance to view in the presence of others. This indulgent sort of introspection pays rich dividends.

During the years I've lived alone I've been presented with a multitude of exciting choices: more ways to feel and think and do and be than I ever imagined in the early stages of being on my own. Knowing that I have complete control over the way I choose to live has given me a sense of power I never thought possible.

In living alone you have the privilege of designing your own lifestyle on the basis of *who you are*. You can choose what your opportunities and relationships will be rather than have either or both forced upon you.

You have the opportunity to grow, to enhance your life, to sort out ideas, to make plans. Because living alone makes you more aware of your options—and because you have more of them in living alone—it becomes a time to make decisions and do the things that you choose to do.

ASSERT YOUR INDEPENDENCE

As a person alone you have a tremendous opportunity to establish true personal independence. Because you must learn to take care of your own needs and to assume total responsibility for yourself without looking to others, you are in a position to acquire the sort of inner strength which results from being your own source of support.

True independence is not easy to achieve. A sense of being complete and whole within yourself doesn't come overnight, believe me. It comes as a result of years of thoughtful, responsible solitary living. Becoming independent also requires that you build a solid confidence in yourself through a series of successful solo ventures: e.g., learning to do things on your own that you may once have required (or desired) the presence of another to do.

Living alone can breed a type of independence which takes root in your sense of self-confidence and grows with your freedom to do as you wish with your life. Once you've known real independence, you will not want to relinquish it. This is not to say that you will never again want to share your life with another. But it does mean that you are more likely to approach any such union with a clearer understanding of who you are, what you have to give, and what you want in return.

BOLSTER YOUR SELF-RELIANCE

Many people who live alone have found a rare form of personal security: the ability to rely entirely upon themselves to meet their own needs. Self-reliance is undoubtedly one of the most important ingredients in a successful life alone.

Becoming self-reliant is its own reward. *There is nothing like knowing for a fact that you can take care of yourself.*

In depending on your own resources for your personal security—in no longer looking to others for what can only come from you—you discover your abilities to be an enormous source of comfort and satisfaction. To be able to say to yourself, "I am a resource of mine; I can depend on me," is most gratifying and tends to be an enhancement to feelings of security and self-esteem.

You discover that no other person can ever give you the security you can't provide yourself, and there is an incredible feeling of personal strength in this knowledge.

If you subscribe to the theory of our essential aloneness as navigators through life's journey, you know that ultimately our only real security is ourselves. What an uplifting feeling to know that you are yours!

FIND PLEASURE IN YOUR PRIVACY AND SOLITUDE

In living alone you are guaranteed the luxury of privacy—a precious indulgence that allows you to remove all guards, to drop all facades, to be completely yourself with yourself and, at the same time, to discover that seclusion has its own delights.

Many people live entire lifetimes never knowing the peace that comes of private moments with oneself. They may grab a few moments here and there, but this means rushing in and out again, never fully knowing or appreciating real solitude. For the person alone, however, it is always there for the taking.

A major advantage attending the privacy of solitary living is that no one can invade it unless permitted. As a loner you are in complete control of this aspect of your life.

To come home to peace and quiet, to

wake up in the morning and be abl… collect your thoughts, to sleep in—undisturbed—at will, to be able to think and create in a peaceful atmosphere, free of interruption—these are but a few of the blessings to be found in the solitude of single living. Retreating into this solitude represents a sort of voluntary exile from the world—an exile in which you can experience complete peace with yourself.

Acquiring an appreciation and enjoyment of solitude can be one of life's peak experiences: learning to be comfortably alone, discovering the pleasure of your own company, making solitude a pleasant state of aloneness—these are yours for the taking when you live alone.

THE TIME IS RIPE

This is a great time to be living on your own. Never before have single people had so many opportunities to create happy, fulfilling lives. Single women are asserting themselves in the job and career markets, while single men are developing their talents on the domestic scene. Books and magazine articles are being written just for them. Seminars, encounter groups, even college classes are conducted expressly for the single person. One has only to glance at the lengthy singles' activities calendars in newspapers to know that there is a lot going one in their quarter.

Whether you've chosen to live alone or not, I hope that in this book you will be able to recognize and capitalize on the advantages intrinsic to the lifestyle—that you will find living alone a very satisfying and fulfilling way to live.

If you have not chosen to live alone, is there any guarantee that your new status as a person alone is a temporary one? Whether it is or isn't, why not strive to make this a good time in your life, regardless of the duration? The challenge of forging a rich and satisfying life alone can be met by anyone who so chooses.

If you are new to living alone, you are beginning a new chapter in your life and will have to make the changes that this new chapter will require. This will take courage, but at the same time it will be exciting. Don't be surprised, in fact, if it turns out to be fun!

THE ADJUSTMENT TO LIVING ALONE

2

Suddenly Alone: Survival 101

Who wakes in a house alone
Wakes to moments of panic.
(Will the roof fall in?
Shall I die today?)
Who wakes in a house alone
Wakes to inertia sometimes,
To fits of weeping for no reason.
Solitude swells the inner space
Like a balloon.
We are wafted hither and thither
On the air currents.
How to land it?

—*MAY SARTON*
"Gestalt at Sixty"

Through the walls of my condominium I hear Beverly's muffled, heartrending sobs. The sister who came to stay following the death of Beverly's husband has gone. Listening to her, I feel that I understand some of the feelings that texture her sobs. She has shared her thoughts with me frequently in her mourning: Bev wishes that she had been the first to die; she would rather be dead than alone. It is, however, a fact of her life that she is very much alive and is going to have to begin to learn to live alone.

Lila calls to say that her husband has left her. (They have been in their new house just one month.) She agonizes, despairs, states categorically that she can not—will not—live alone. Together we explore her situation and discover that at this particular time in her life she has no other alternative.

SURVIVING THE FIRST FEW DAYS (WEEKS, MONTHS)

When the essence of your existence—the use of your time and energy, the determination of your priorities—has been built around another person, it can be a most difficult thing to learn to live on your own. Always to have thought of yourself in relation to another and then to find yourself suddenly alone forces you to begin to shape a new role in life, to establish new priorities. For many these are not easy tasks.

Coming home to an empty house, eating alone, sleeping alone—all these mean adjusting to a new way of life. For many people the experience of living alone after separation, divorce or widowhood is the first such experience in their lives. These individuals may find adjusting particularly difficult. They have been accustomed to the continual presence of another person.

These people imagine, in their grief, that they can never find compensation for the losses they have suffered. When they find it necessary, after a while, to turn their attentions to the practical aspects of their lives, many acknowledge a sense of helplessness about such things—about setting up house, about adapting to a foreign lifestyle, about learning what to do with their time.

The initial phase of living alone is often as especially trying time for these individuals in that they are experiencing emotional chaos at the very time they are attempting to adapt to an unfamiliar lifestyle. If a physical move is required, the person may come under a great deal of additional stress.

Often budget and finances must be rearranged and can be sources of great concern. Establishing a new social life worries many; others express a lack of trust in the future and are unwilling to believe that there is anything to which they may look forward.

A myriad of concerns, problems, questions, worries, fears and doubts confronts these individuals just when they feel most vulnerable and are apt to be most unsure of themselves emotionally. Unfortunately, the "friendly" divorce or separation makes it no less difficult to go out and find a place and begin to rebuild.

As one forty-year-old man lamented in the wake of his divorce, "The last thing I ever expected in life was to have to learn to take care of myself."

Divorce, separation and widowhood come with heavy pressures. In personal relationships, losses that are or may be permanent are difficult to accept. For fate to demand that we adjust simultaneously to the loss of a mate and to living alone seems cruel. Awash in feelings of profound sadness and disorientation, it is enough just to keep our heads above water. It is not uncommon at this point to feel paralyzed and frightened enough to believe that we can't possibly face life alone.

Such was the case for Dorothy P.: "The first year following my divorce I was so crazy, it's a wonder they didn't lock me up. Nothing about me was normal. My life was in total confusion. I couldn't make decisions; I didn't have the will to do anything. I felt like half a pair of scissors and functioned just as effectively."

The person left suddenly alone is often overtaken by a confusing variety of emotions: numbness, resentment, self-pity, anger, guilt, anxiety, depression. At the height of these feelings, while still in the midst of emotional upheaval, the enormity of being alone strikes.

Some lodge an angry protest against the unfairness of life and against those they feel are more fortunate. Some feel so despondent, and at such an utter loss, that for them life seems pointless. Decisions are made in haste and changes are instituted prematurely. Suicides are contemplated and sometimes carried out. But most people, given the support of family and friends, as well as the passage of time, do survive and do bounce back, recovering both their happiness and their sense of purpose.

Individuals who are adjusting to living alone must learn to cope with their feelings and to recognize that in time these feelings will pass. Taking care of yourself is an acquired skill. You must learn to develop your survival skills and strategies along the way. As an example, many people who are new to living alone find just coming home difficult. The quiet emptiness of their residences seems to reflect the emptiness of their lives. Some go home as seldom as possible, while others don't go home at all.

An acquaintance of mine spent the first year and a half following his divorce away from his apartment. So abhorrent to him was the thought of spending an evening alone that he literally ran away from it. He scheduled dinner engagements nightly, came home on occasion to sleep, and, once a month or so, stayed long enough to dust the place and tidy up a bit. The irony is that, because he prolonged the inevitable, his life alone got off to a needlessly slow and disadvantaged start.

Developing self-sufficiency, achieving emotional independence, mastering the mechanics of everyday living, mustering needed emotional support, getting yourself "together"—all are important priorities for the person suddenly confronted with having to live alone. You may not be able to change the fact that you are alone, but you certainly *can* exercise some control over the way in which you approach your new way of life.

THE ADJUSTMENT PROCESS

Finding ways to get past the first few days, weeks and months of living alone is of paramount importance to the novice. While there are many methods of adapting and coping, the need which they have been designed to meet is one which is lodged in a very basic question: *How can I survive the worst of all possible human conditions?*

The need to adjust is especially critical when a change in lifestyle has caused feelings of bewilderment, lethargy and disorientation to take root. Some people report feeling panicky and frightened of being alone; others complain of restlessness and an inability to concentrate which prevents them from enjoying former hobbies and interests. Some feel a desperate need to be with other people. These strange, fluctuating and often disturbing feelings must be recognized by the individual; only then will he be on the road to conquering them and regaining control over his life.

Before we get into the specific steps which can be taken to ease the adjustment process, a question worth considering presents itself: Is the adjustment process more difficult for men than for their female counterparts?

While this question has been posed to me on several occasions, it seems to me that there is no clear-cut answer; so much depends on the individual and on what he brings to his situation. Some men are able to take care of themselves very well, while others who may never have acquired certain fundamental domestic skills are likely to encounter a few difficulties in their efforts to create a home for themselves. These men speak of feeling awkward in the supermarket, of not knowing how to sew or launder—"buy new rather than do" becomes their motto. Cooking presents its own problems, making it a task which is easier to avoid than to tackle.

To be forced to learn to take care of yourself and your home when you've never had to do either certainly can complicate and perhaps prolong the adjustment process. Of course, there is no reason why you can't enjoy the experience of learning to care for yourself in the ways we've discussed, even though you may not have chosen to do so.

Male or female, domestic skills or no, the following steps will go a long way toward helping you not only survive the adjustment process, but come out stronger and better for it as well.

Understanding and Accepting Your Condition

Most people new to living alone begin on a coping basis—not tackling and solving problems, but just living one day to the next. For many these are uncertain and uneven times, full of ups and downs. However in order to cultivate a life alone that offers enriching options, you have to move beyond the coping phase. This is easy to say but sometimes difficult to do. For some, just learning to cope is a major accomplishment; building further in the early stages is out of the question. Ultimately, however, you must begin to build, and a good place to start is in the areas of acceptance and self-reliance.

Living alone and its potential problems must be met with the strengths and resources of each individual. Each of us brings different things to our particular situations, but we all have one thing to call our own: ourselves. It is this very self with which we must deal in order to make a satisfactory adjustment to living alone.

One of the first things you must do is to *accept your aloneness.* Then—and this is where self-reliance comes in—you must resolve not to allow it to get the better of you. Acknowledge your circumstances and make a commitment to yourself to succeed. Refuse to accept the idea of failure or defeat from the start. Challenge yourself to survive it! Remind yourself that you are your own first and last resource. In other words, you can best begin by immediately accepting the responsibility for your own happiness.

Whether you like it or not, you have to muster your own support. Friends and family can help, but solid support must ultimately come from within. This does not mean that you must be a paragon of strength and resolution from day one. On the contrary, you can expect to be waylaid at times by feelings of anger or grief or self-doubt. Your only "rule" in the beginning is to live one day to the next until you feel prepared to accept the challenge of building a new life for yourself.

You must learn to work through your feelings, to accept them as natural and normal. Remember, you have a lot of company—one-fifth of the population. Others have doubted they would survive, but they have learned to accept their situations and have bounced back just as you can.

Some people take longer to adjust than do others. It is important that you be aware of this and that you *give yourself time.* Rather than make decisions impulsively or out of fear, wait until your feelings have stabilized and you are feeling more secure about your future. If you are especially unsettled, it is a good idea to postpone major decision making. Don't try to resolve everything at once. Time is on your side. It is a great healer, capable of reducing anxieties and resolving uncertainties. Things that may seem overwhelming now will not always be so.

Though many specific suggestions are made in later chapters to help ease the transition to your new lifestyle, these are the guidelines for a satisfactory adjustment at this point: to try to accept the present, to delay making major decisions, to know that the passage of time will only help. Unfortunately, you can't always be in control of the circumstances which change your life. What do you do when the rug is pulled out from under you? Simple: You get back up again.

Facing Your Demons

Learning to deal with your fears, worries and doubts is the necessary second step in adjusting to living alone.

Many people who live alone, even when they've chosen to, approach single living with a good many apprehensions. The greatest fear they have seems to revolve around self-sufficiency: *What if I can't stand on my own two feet?*

A secondary worry for some, primary for others, involves financial security: *Am I capable of providing myself a satisfactory means of support?*

Another very common concern haunts many: *What if I become ill? Who will take care of me?* For some the worries seem unending: *Will I starve to death? Will I be able to sleep?*

Finally, the worst fear: *What if I have to spend the rest of my life this way?*

For those of you who are living alone for the first time in your lives, especially if you are doing so against your wishes, moving toward a healthy acceptance of your situation may take a great deal of time. It is wise, therefore, to begin to allay your fears by dealing with each one singularly, so as not to be overwhelmed by the lot of them.

The first step is to identify each fear as

precisely as possible. If you can call something by its name, you can deal with it. The more precise you can be in identifying and analyzing each fear, the greater will be your chances for overcoming it. As you begin to identify your fears, it is important that you attempt to play devil's advocate with them. Perhaps the other side is not as terrible as imagined. This sort of exercise is effective in helping you keep your fears in proper perspective.

Remember, if you can acknowledge your fears, you will be free of having to hide from them or from the realities which produce them.

Developing a Realistic Perspective

Blowing your fears out of proportion can only serve to compound your misery. Keeping things in realistic perspective with regard to your situation is the third important step in making a successful adjustment to living alone. Reality can sometimes smack you right between the eyes, tempting you to avoid it altogether; but to avoid coming to grips with your situation is only to risk the paying of a higher price later on.

There are specific things which you can do in order to develop and maintain a realistic perspective, and some of them are listed here:

—Don't allow yourself to be overcome by the enormity of your situation. Others have gone before you and have survived; so will you.

—Try to put your aloneness in the perspective of being part of your life—and only *one* part of your life. Try not to see it as an engulfing, consuming thing that may ultimately destroy you.

—Expect to cope with your life on a day-to-day basis in the beginning. Learn to endure, to live as well as you can from one day to the next.

—Know that living alone can be a mixture of freedom, fear, anxiety, instability and loneliness, but that it can be managed and can promise some rewards.

—Be aware that a plan made in a positive frame of mind is more likely to be followed than one conceived in desperation.

—Recognize that while you can expect some help from others, most of the important work will have to be done by you.

—Remember that the process of learning to live alone can take a long time.

—Learn to accept your aloneness as a potentially permanent condition of your life. (This possibility alone makes your need for a successful adjustment critical.)

Mark G., a young man who found the going very rough when his wife first left him, acknowledges that he has finally begun to keep his head above water.

"The worst time," he says, "is at night when no one is here. But I know now that the only thing to do is to live through it. The sun *will* come up tomorrow. Another day *will* dawn."

Learning to be realistic in your approach to the inevitable—learning to "guts it" through a trying time if you have to—will take you a long way down the road toward living alone and liking it.

THE MINUTE-BY-MINUTE APPROACH TO SURVIVAL

Working your way into a system of day-to-day living will eventually lead you to a broader approach to the single lifestyle. Adjusting to living alone, as adjusting to anything in life, is best accomplished one step at a time. The people who live alone most happily seem to be those whose independence is joined with a sense of purpose. It is here that the value of planning comes in.

How do I begin again? is a question asked by many who have found themselves alone after years of living with others. For them, mastering the mechanics of everyday living can present a real challenge. Building a solid base for the new life into which you've been thrust takes time, but it can be accomplished more easily if you begin by restructuring in simple ways.

For certain individuals living by themselves for the first time—people who previously have centered their lives around another individual or family—a sense of normal activity is lost. For some of these "lost souls," however, careful daily planning can help offset the uncertainties of sudden freedom.

Planning is needed to circumvent lonely periods, to give meaning and definition to life, and to provide things to which one may look forward. Both short-term and long-range planning have great value for the person adjusting to living alone.

Structurring a life for one may be one of the most difficult and challenging tasks with which a person is faced in the initial stages of living alone. Among the people I interviewed, most confessed to having some difficulty adjusting to living alone, even if they'd chosen it as a lifestyle. Of course the degrees of difficulty varied with the individuals; however, I did find a common thread among those who found themselves suddenly alone as a result of death, separation or divorce. Most reported that they were floudering, unable to cope with living by themselves months after that had begun.

After learning to accept their new condition, individuals who find themselves suddenly alone and are having difficulty adjusting must learn to arrange the components of their day-to-day lives in a more satisfying way. This can be accomplished in part by setting up a schedule for daily living and sticking to it.

The kinds of activities which comprise the schedule are less significant at the start than is the structuring of the schedule itself. If your internal world is chaotic, keeping a schedule in the outer world should help. It can give you a sense of order, something to hold onto. It can also help to stem the aimless, floating feeling that troubles many newcomers to living alone.

Janet H., a young designer who was caught by surprise when her husband requested a divorce, found herself totally unprepared for a life alone.

"None of the things I used to do to fill my time appeals to me now," she told me. "I hate to go home to an empty apartment, so I've taken to trying to fill my life with work. I know I have to get used to living by myself sooner or later, but I just don't know how or where to start."

As we talked I stressed to her the importance of learning to live in your surroundings as soon as you possibly can. Avoiding doing so only seems to prolong the agony, so to speak, and eventually you are bound to come face to face with yourself with very little to show for the time spent running away. The sooner you can get yourself established, the better off you'll be.

I recommended to Janet that she leave work on time the next day. Together we planned a schedule of activities which were appealing to her and which we hoped would carry her successfully through the evening. In the course of our planning we both realized that she needed minute-by-minute guidance, so we set it up this way:

5:00 Stop on the way home and shop for dinner ingredients. Choose anything that is appealing.
5:30 Prepare dinner.
6:00 Eat dinner; clean up.
6:30 Read the evening newspaper.
7:00 Watch television.
9:00 Soak in a hot tub.
9:30 Crawl into bed with a book or magazine.

When I saw Janet a week or so later she reported that during her coffee break each day she had made up a schedule for that evening. She said that she was spending more time at home and was beginning to enjoy it more. She also reported that sticking to her schedule had helped to keep her from dwelling exclusively on her problems.

You may or may not require such detailed structuring to help you in adjusting to living alone. The point here is that it worked for Janet and helped her get started on the road toward a more successful and rewarding experience.

Setting up some sort of schedule for

day-to-day living seems to be especially helpful to people who have previously structured their living routines around another person or around family members. Such a schedule seems to help eliminate a lot of anxiety and time wasted brooding about one's condition.

Mary B., a recent widow, says, "I make it through the week just fine; I have my job, and it keeps me busy. But the weekends are my undoing. If I don't have something specific lined up, the time hangs heavy on my hands and I wind up getting very depressed."

In order to help Mary reverse this pattern, we first divided her weekends into six major blocks of time: Saturday morning, afternoon and evening, and Sunday morning, afternoon and evening. The purpose of this was to give her a fairly loose framework within which to make plans for those times when she had "nothing to do."

The next step for Mary was to decide how to fill each block of time productively. She arrived at this:

SATURDAY

MORNING	AFTERNOON	EVENING
Clean apartment	Window shop	Watch TV
Do marketing	Go out for lunch	Read book or magazine
	Lounge by the pool	

SUNDAY

MORNING	AFTERNOON	EVENING
Fix brunch	Do Sunday crossword puzzle	Visit with daughter or friends
Read Sunday paper	Sunbathe on patio	
Do indoor gardening		

The purpose of this sort of detailed structuring was twofold: to establish an organized plan for a period of time which she had found difficult to handle, and to give her some security in the knowledge that she did have something planned on the weekends.

After following her new plan for several weeks, Mary told me that she was no longer approaching the weekend with dread, nor was she beginning each week with the feelings of emptiness and depression she had once had. She is now at the point where she can spend a pleasant weekend at home by herself, reading and engaging in other activities without becoming depressed. More important, she seems to be well on her way to becoming a whole person again.

What works for one person will not necessarily work for another. The preceding examples worked for the individuals involved, but they may not work for you. While there is no patent formula guaranteed to work for everyone, there is a good chance that a schedule which has been formulated with your needs and interests in mind can be of great assistance to you in your adjustment to living alone.

IF I CHOOSE TO LIVE ALONE, WILL I HAVE PROBLEMS ADJUSTING?

One might assume that if a person *chooses* to live alone, the adjustment period must be relatively easy, if not nonexistent. Though this happens sometimes, such is not always the case. Some people who have longed for freedom don't know exactly what to do with it once they've got it. Wanting to be free and knowing how to handle freedom when it is acquired are two different things. Learning how to manage your freedom is an important part of learning to live alone.

Even people who plan religiously for the

day when they can occupy places of their own can have difficulty adjusting to living by themselves once their plans become reality. Few, if any, of us have the opportunity to experience living by ourselves during the developmental years between infancy and graduation from high school. Most of us are part of a structured social unit, usually the family. Learning to live outside that unit takes some getting used to, as Kay L. can testify:

"I grew up in a large family—so large that I never had a room of my own. When I was in college, living in the crowded dormitory, I used to dream of the day when I would move into an apartment of my very own—have complete privacy, decorate the place the way I wanted to, live the way I wanted to, the whole thing. When my dream finally came true, though, my bubble seemed to burst. I didn't know what to do with myself. I felt lost. In fact, the quiet nearly drove me crazy."

Kay's disorientation, though she couldn't know it at the time, was natural. You can't expect to go from living with people to living alone without experiencing *some* feelings of confusion or bewilderment. It's finding a way to get through those feelings that is important. Kay goes on:

"I was very proud and determined to make it a successful experience. I had bragged about having a place of my own for so long that I couldn't very well go crawling back home. After a lot of hard thinking—after being scared and having tremendous misgivings—I decided to key in on one of the aspects of my dream and go to work on it. I began to spend entire days shopping for items to use in decorating the apartment. The next thing I knew I was a thoroughly involved 'interior decorator.' The project took me about six months to complete, and by then I was enjoying living by myself just as I'd imagined I would."

One of the secrets, then, is to give yourself some specific direction at the very outset. It's also important to anticipate some sort of adjustment period and to prepare for it. Together these may help prevent the "lost" feeling that can occur.

Another example of someone's choosing to live alone and then experiencing difficulty adjusting arose during an interview with a gentleman named Jim S. Jim had ended a twenty-five-year marriage so that he could "live the way he'd always wanted to."

As he tells it, "Helen's and my living habits were diametrically opposed. I figured that if I got out on my own, I could live better; I wouldn't have another person's interference.

"As an example, I love to get up early in the morning and read. For twenty-five years Helen complained about how much it disturbed her. I began to relish the idea of indulging my habit without having to listen to my wife's objections.

"On the other side of the coin, she had a habit that annoyed the socks off me. Every single night of the year she fell asleep on the couch in front of the television. In my dream of having a place of my own, Helen wasn't sleeping on the couch."

Jim purchased a condominium unit before a divorce action was even initiated. That's how determined and sure he was that living by himself was what he wanted to do. Much to his surprise and dismay, however, moving into the new place was one of the loneliest things he'd ever done. The next thing he knew he was calling his almost ex-wife on the phone and begging her to come for a visit. Having his own place had very quickly lost its glamor.

What it got down to was that Jim could not get used to the absence of a daily routine. There was no breakfast time per se, no dinner time, no set time for anything.

"I couldn't seem to regulate my life," he continued, "and all of a sudden Helen's 'bad habits' didn't seem so bad. I gave up and asked her to move in, hoping that her presence would provide the structure my life was missing. She agreed and the divorce papers were withdrawn."

Within a month all the old annoyances had resurfaced; at the end of six weeks Jim and his wife separated for good.

"It was at that point that I realized I had to establish my own routines if I was going to make it on my own. It was one of the most difficult challenges of my life, but I managed—slowly. And, to be honest, there were times when I would backslide and think I wasn't going to make it."

One of the first things Jim did was to start inviting friends over for brunch on weekends and dinner on week nights. The shopping and planning required for entertaining helped build a routine into his life. Before long he didn't have to depend on company to help schedule his existence; he could do it himself.

Sometimes the opposite happens: the first few months of freedom and indulgence are so glorious that you can't imagine you'll ever *not* like living alone. Laura T., a woman now in her early thirties, first took an apartment by herself when she was twenty-four. She had been out of college for two years and had lived with rommates during that time. When she accepted a newspaper job in a city where she knew no one, she had no choice but to live alone.

"Everything about the experience seemed exotic to me at first. I was intoxicated by the bravery and maturity I thought I had exhibited in saying goodbye to everyone and everything I knew in order to take a job in an unfamiliar city. Because the job required that I work odd hours, living alone had 'perfect' written all over it. I could come in at two or three in the morning and not disturb anyone. I could play my stereo, read until the sun came up, and sleep until noon—without anyone's disturbing me.

"This 'heaven-on-earth' condition reigned uninterrupted for about eleven months—until I sat up in bed one night with a lump in my throat and realized I was lonely. That's not to say that living alone soured for me at that moment. All that happened was the euphoria gave way to something more real—a way of living that for me is about ninety per cent wonderful and ten per cent tough."

For Laura the need to adjust did not make itself known until she had lived alone for almost a year. By that time she knew so well what she liked about living alone that she was willing to do whatever she found necessary in order to maintain her lifestyle and her balance and wholeness as a human being too.

YOU ARE YOUR OWN BEST ASSET

The ability to make the most of your resources is a valuable asset under any of life's conditions, and it seems to be particularly important in the adjustment to living alone. What else is there? Better yet, who else is there? Because we are never guaranteed the continuing support of another in our lives, we must take the responsibility for learning to care for ourselves.

The adjustment to living alone may necessitate a realignment or restructuring of your priorities. It may require you to find other directions for yourself and to seek out new and constructive pathways. If former roles have been lost or rejected, new ones must be developed. Perhaps new relationships must be formed or new social environments established.

Whatever challenges must be met, living alone can provide many opportunities for personal growth, the best of which may be the opportunity to recreate yourself—to build a stronger and more enduring sense of your personal identity than you may ever have been allowed to construct previously. You may indeed develop a formula for living that is designed specifically to meet your needs. Moreover, you may come to understand what it means to live alone successfully: When faced with difficult and trying circumstances that might once have threatened your undoing, you do not fall victim to self-pity or catastrophic expectations. With the passage of time your coping skills will have evolved to the extent that you are able to handle difficult situations with a combination of cheerfulness and efficiency. And, believe me, you will take pride in the increasing competence with which you are able to plan and oversee your new life.

3

Combating Loneliness

Although living alone can stimulate the presence of loneliness in your life, it is possible to live alone with a minimum amount of it—to transform *loneliness* into a comfortable state of *aloneness.* There is a difference.

While *aloneness* denotes simply being by yourself, *loneliness* implies a longing for companionship—a wish not to be alone. The problem is that many consider the terms interchangeable: Being alone automatically means being lonely.

This need not be so. If being alone is a fact of your life, then being lonely can be minimized to an extent you may not have thought possible.

Bear in mind first that loneliness is not new. It is an age-old condition. While it may not be possible for you to overcome loneliness altogether, lonely experiences can be managed to a point where they actually can be turned into something of value.

Second, know that loneliness is nondiscriminatory. It can attack anyone anywhere. Many people who live alone are no lonelier than unhappily married people whose loneliness may be accentuated by an unsatisfactory union. Ironically, often the worst kind of loneliness is experienced in the company of another person.

Many busy, independent people have no time to feel lonely, but for others who may have been separated from a partner, loneliness can be a hazard—a fearful thing with which they would rather not have to contend. Most of all, they fear that they might lose control over the symptoms—symptoms which may include feeling physically ill, mentally unstable, and, perhaps worse, terribly deprived. This seeming unfairness may cause one at times to feel abandoned, angry or bitter. Agonizing feelings of worthlessness and failure often accompany a lonely experience.

Said one young man, describing how he'd felt after being rejected by his lover, "I thought that life was all over for me. I was sure that no one had ever been as lonely as I was."

Loneliness is painful. It hurts beyond all hurts at times. Feelings of emotional emptiness brought on by loneliness can cause you to think strange thoughts and do strange things. To many, loneliness signifies a monster which threatens their undoing and certainly precludes any possibility of living alone and liking it. The threat of loneliness floats over the heads of these people like a black cloud, capable of unleashing an uncontrollable flood of anxiety and pain. People often tend to feel overwhelmed by the scope of the problem of loneliness and pessimistic about their ability to combat it effectively.

If the number one problem for you in living alone is loneliness, how do you ward off the pain that it causes? How do you deal with the problem of time hanging heavy on your hands? How do you compensate for the feeling that something is missing in your life? When feelings of loneliness tend to snowball, how do you manage to control your fears?

There are as many answers to these questions as there are people dealing with them. While loneliness as an individual problem requires an individual solution, there are many things you can do to combat it on both a personal and a social level, the most important of which are explored in this and subsequent chapters. Realistically speaking, I can't promise you a cure, but perhaps I can make the symptoms tolerable.

If I Close My Eyes, Will It Go Away?

Who, given a choice, wants to be faced with being lonely? Because combating loneliness demands that you draw upon your strongest inner resources, it seems easier to avoid the challenge altogether. Whether you should tackle loneliness by plunging into work, by getting involved in social activities, by keeping busy, or whether you should confront the nature of your loneliness directly is a critical decision which faces every person who lives alone.

While there is no doubt that dealing with loneliness directly is truly challenging and, if successful, enormously rewarding, is it also true that loneliness can be alleviated by keeping yourself so busy that you forget your predicament? Probably not. I suspect that unless you learn to deal with loneliness whenever it confronts you, it will only come back to haunt you later—and its impact may be doubled.

Perhaps we should examine a few of the reasons why some people will go to extremes to avoid facing the experience of being lonely. In the first place, we know that an instinctive response to loneliness is fear. We also know that, as human beings, we tend to fear that which we do not know.

The fact that loneliness can cause pain is enough to scare some people, and understandably so. Frantic attempts to avoid it may stem from a fear of losing control over some of the effects of loneliness—feelings of "illness," instability, emptiness, longing or deprivation. Where loneliness is concerned, so many people are so busy running from it, they never stop to identify what it is, exactly, or why it produces such fear. Running from distraction to distraction seems somehow easier than looking loneliness in the eye.

Finally, loneliness is something to which none of us likes to admit—either to ourselves or to others. We feel it implies that we are somehow lacking. In truth, it is very difficult to express the feelings of worthlessness and failure that can accompany loneliness. We do not want others to know how we feel for fear that they will take advantage of our weakness or, worse, confirm our feelings of low self-esteem. It is easier to construct a protective, confident front.

In spite of denials, however, the feelings of anxiety and failure will persist, emphasizing the need for us to learn to come to terms with the loneliness that is sometimes a part of being alone.

Unfortunately, there is no way out of loneliness but through it. To go around it means to risk being overtaken by it later on. It seems like a much better idea to meet it head-on, analyze it, understand it, grapple with it, and make it your ally. Acknowledging rather than denying it seems to make it much easier to deal with.

Rather than regard it as a shameful emotion, realize that loneliness is a human emotion. If you can just bring yourself to say, "I am lonely," you will have taken a big first step toward winning your own personal battle with loneliness.

PHASE ONE: LETTING YOURSELF EXPERIENCE LONELINESS

The common tendency for most of us is not only to avoid our own loneliness, but to come to the rescue of someone we perceive as being in the grip of a lonely experience. Certainly it is difficult to stand by when we feel someone is suffering, but sometimes our desire to help has a harmful effect. The result is that we inadvertently deny that person an opportunity for building strength and character—an important outgrowth of the struggle to understand and respond to one's own loneliness.

Learning to deal with loneliness is an art. It may be one of the biggest challenges any of us faces in life. The value in confronting loneliness directly was mentioned previously, and it remains the best place to start:

—*Face it.* Don't be afraid to acknowledge what you are feeling. The fact is that you can't do anything to alleviate the problem until you have first recognized what it is that's troubling you.

—*Accept it.* Know that there are times and situations in everyone's life which produce feelings of loneliness—whether others are willing to admit to this or not. A certain amount of loneliness in one's life is to be expected.

Don't try to escape it by running away from it; such an approach will only make it worse later on. Don't wallow in it or panic at the feelings which it engenders. Take time to examine its effects on you and make some decisions as to what you can do about it.

—*Manage it.* Much of the distress and fear of loneliness will be diminished when you can identify what causes the problem and then attempt to modify the conditions which produce your lonely feelings. Whenever I feel lonely for companionship, for example, I find that inviting a friend to dinner or suggesting that we dine out will brighten my spirits immediately.

The Two Faces of Loneliness

Loneliness seems to present itself to me in two different ways. There are times when lonely feelings strike quickly and seemingly at random. When this occurs I find them easy to dispel. Often simple action—a slight modification in my plans for the moment—is enough to turn things around.

The second way in which loneliness strikes is somewhat more difficult to combat. Rather than surfacing suddenly and departing on cue, this form, which seems to manifest itself as a *period of loneliness*, grows more furtively, is more difficult to detect, and does not respond as readily to treatment. Getting rid of this kind of loneliness requires a bit more planning.

I remember noticing, when living alone was new to me, the development of a very definite "loneliness pattern" on days when I wasn't working. The hours that passed from the time I finished my chores—usually about mid-afternoon—until dinner time were consistently very lonely ones for me.

Perhaps boredom contributed to my loneliness, or maybe it was caused by the lack of someone with whom to interact. Whatever it was, I didn't sit through too many of those miserable spells before I realized that I had to do something about them.

From that point of awareness on, I always planned something fun for this potentially lonely time. Sometimes I went visiting or bookstore browsing. Other times I tried my hand at baking, or took in a movie, or went shopping for gourmet foods. No more sitting around feeling bad and wondering what was wrong.

Once you have identified what it is that makes you feel lonely, you are in a better position to deal with it. Take note of your loneliness when you sense it and try to discover what prompted the feeling. When you can pinpoint the cause of your loneliness, it isn't hard to find ways to handle it.

Often the simplest act can alleviate the problem.

—*Use it.* Transform loneliness into something of value to you. Turn it to your advantage by learning to handle it on your own, thus enhancing your self-reliance—your most important asset as a person alone. Use it as an opportunity to know yourself better, to gauge your thoughts, feelings and perceptions. Look upon lonely times as opportunities for personal growth rather than as dreadful periods to be suffered through.

Once you have acquired the art of dealing with loneliness, you will find yourself "breaking through" feelings of panic and self-pity into a kind of calm and self-assurance that will surprise you. The investment of positive emotional energy in overcoming loneliness will pay off in the long run.

It is hard work; it demands purposeful activity—not escapism. In fact, passivity on your part will more than likely only intensify your feelings of loneliness.

Finally, remember that conquering certain aspects of loneliness does not guarantee that you will not experience it again. But when you do, the ability to face it, accept it, manage it, and use it to your advantage will make it easier and less painful each time.

Self-Discovery and Personal Growth

Beyond the first pangs of despair, can a lonely experience provide you an opportunity for personal growth? Can it at the same time provide an impetus to self-discovery? When you are suffering the pain that a lonely experience can bring, it would hardly seem possible that you could expect to profit by it emotionally. On the contrary, many suspect at such a time that their emotional selves have regressed to a point of no return.

From my own battle with loneliness I have come to believe two things: that surviving periods of loneliness can give you greater self-assurance, and that efforts to escape the experience of loneliness can deprive you of an important avenue of personal growth.

Just knowing that you can face a lonely experience and come out on the other side can be a real confidence builder. The sense of pleasure that results from developing a tolerance of loneliness and ultimately mastering a lonely experience is very rewarding.

I believe that learning to combat loneliness effectively has contributed more to my growth as a person than any other single thing in my life. It has been a maturing experience for me that is unequaled in caliber.

This is not to say that I no longer experience loneliness or that, when I do, dealing with it is always easy. It's just that knowing that I can have control over it instead of its having control over me gives me a feeling of strength that is very reassuring.

Though you may not have thought of it in this way, you can use your periods of loneliness to discover more about yourself and your life. Exploring your loneliness can take you right to the heart of your inner self. Constructive searching into that self will allow you to know yourself in a more intimate way than ever before.

I use the word *constructive* here very deliberately. It is too tempting, when you're feeling down and out and bad about yourself, to turn your hurt and anger on your most convenient target: you. No worthwhile purpose is served in naming yourself the most despicable person you know. Use this time instead to peer into yourself in as fair and detached a way as possible, giving credit where credit is due and owning up to weaknesses where they exist.

You have the chance at such a time to paint a unique self-portrait—one in which you will see reflected your own humanness: illogical feelings, inconsistencies, foibles and conflicts. You will discover at the same time talents, values, convictions and strengths. You might well become conscious of personal resources and capabilites of which you were not previously aware.

Self-knowledge is, I think, necessary to anyone who wishes to find meaning in life, to grow as a person, or to realize his full potential as a human being. Why not take advantage of the lonely periods in your life to know yourself in a fuller and more honest way than before?

If your experience is anything like mine, this newly acquired self-knowledge can open the way to more meaningful human relationships and to a greater valuing of all aspects of life. This voyage of self-discovery can expand your social and personal horizons as well as usher in a more meaningful life experience for you.

In living alone you are inevitably cut off from constant human companionship. However, experiencing solitary living gives you the opportunity to draw upon untouched capacities and resources and to know yourself in an entirely unique way.

Periods of loneliness can be filled with pain and fear, yet they can also provide opportunities for greater self-awareness, for developing yourself as a person, and for perceiving life in a new and different manner.

The personal torment which sometimes accompanies loneliness can, if managed properly, be the beginning of a rewarding experience of self-discovery, a key to deeper personal insights and a warmer appreciation of life.

PHASE TWO: TURNING LONELINESS AROUND

There is another dimension to dealing with loneliness which is somewhat opposed to the idea of immersing oneself in it, understanding it, grappling with it, and emerging victorious. In no way is the discussion of this added dimension intended to diminish the importance of meeting loneliness head-on and dealing with it in a direct and personal way. It is, instead, like putting a cap on a bottle or adding a finishing touch. I call it the *Triple-A Approach:*

1. Maintain a good *attitude;* have positive expectations.
2. Take an *aggressive* approach to your own loneliness problem.
3. Begin to pursue new, creative, enjoyable *activities* that do not require the presence of another person.

There is no doubt that at times one who lives alone gets sick and tired of being alone. Monotony sets in and is sometimes followed by depression; the two combined can greatly compound the loneliness problem for many people. Happily, there *are* things you can do to make yourself feel better when and if you reach this stage.

The Importance of Attitude

It all begins with attitude. The way you choose to look at something has a direct bearing upon how you will be affected by it. One of the most valuable pieces of advice ever given me was during an incident in my life when I felt I had been used to poor advantage by a partner in a business deal. The advice was simple: Restructure your thinking with regard to the whole incident.

This may sound pat to the extent of being meaningless, but, believe it or not, I directed the emphasis in my thinking away from the negative to the positive aspects of the situation and never looked back. Something that sounded like a slogan had been converted into a reality. The little dark cloud over my head drifted away.

There have been numerous times in my life when the ability to restructure my thinking has made a positive contribution in a negative situation. I agree with those who say if you expect the worst, it's sure to happen. But even when it does, there is still time to lessen any devastating effects by refusing to dwell on whatever negatives may be involved.

When dealing with the critical problem of loneliness in your life, it is important to maintain a positive attitude and to hold positive expectations for the outcome. Remember that attitude is everything and that restructuring your thinking to emphasize the positive elements in a given situation can be very beneficial.

Taking an Aggressive Approach

Taking an aggressive approach to your own loneliness problem is the important second step in getting a grip on loneliness. Sometimes loneliness can make you feel lethargic—as though you don't want to do anything. Usually this can be remedied just by starting to do something—preferably something you like.

Before I learned to deal with the loneliness-lethargy syndrome, there were times when it really got the best of me. The lethargy would evolve into a state of apathy so intense that it might linger for days at a time. At first I wasn't able even to identify what was wrong, but I did notice on a couple of occasions that when I was forced out of the doldrums by outside influences, my attitude improved immediately, my energy returned and I felt like a new person.

From those experiences I drew a simple conclusion: If I felt so much better when I was forced out of a lethargic state, why couldn't I create my own "force" and thereby avoid falling into the trap in the first place? It wasn't long before I was able to recognize the symptoms and make the choice to take immediate action.

Even on those occasions when nothing really appealed to me, I made sure to do something. That something could be as simple and unglamorous as dusting the furniture or putting myself in my car and going for a drive. Once I had taken the initial action, my thinking was reoriented and I felt better.

The continuing success of forcing activity as one means of dealing with loneliness led me to the position of advocating an aggressive approach to combating the problem. A very eligible bachelor confided to me once that his worst problem in living alone was having to put up with the occasional bouts of loneliness.

These recurring episodes got him down until, as he put it, "I used my tennis racquet to ward off the problem. Whenever I felt a bout of loneliness coming on, I got out the old racquet and either challenged someone to a match or served the ball against a wall. That sort of aggressive approach really helped me."

I know this may sound like an oversimplified approach to what can be a very complex and trying problem, but if the suffering individual can narrow it down to a simple choice—I can either wallow in my loneliness or I can choose to do something about it—a new direction can be found and much suffering can be eliminated.

As my grandmother used to say, "A change of activity can turn your mind." Even if you have only the slightest interest in something, act on it.

CREATING AND MAINTAINING YOUR OWN SOCIAL SUPPORTS

One of the greatest needs for the person alone is the need for human contact. The importance of such contact cannot be overstated. It is essential in helping to maintain one's balance as a mentally healthy human being. Sometimes the absence of such contact brings on feelings of loneliness that are difficult to deal with.

An aggressive approach can help here, too. Too many lonely people wait for others to contact them. For some the wait is long and the feelings of loneliness only compound themselves.

In our highly mobile society many families no longer live within the same restricted geographical boundaries they once did. Today's extended family is often scattered across the land, leaving many people stranded in geographical areas miles away from one another.

Many small towns which once gave a person alone a feeling of friendly social support have blended into larger, more impersonal suburbs. People today seem to be more reluctant to reach out and help provide social support to the person alone; consequently that person must often muster his or her own support.

This means having to take responsibility for the construction of your own social network—having to go out and find supportive people and build supportive relationships.

Irene R., a recently widowed woman, confided to me that she had been consulting a psychologist in order to help her deal with her loneliness. The psychologist had told her that her problem could be attributed directly to a "lack of extended family" in her area.

She lived on the West Coast and every member of her family, except for one daughter, lived on the eastern seaboard. Her job would not permit her to move to be near them, so the only choice that remained for her was to structure her own social supports.

No matter how well you adapt to living alone, there will always be times when you are alone and want to be with others. That's where the importance of friends comes in. Aside from providing companionship and being a confidant, a good friend can be a source of emotional support unlike any other. We often fail to realize that many of our needs for love and understanding can be met within our friendships.

A friend can help make decisions and share feelings, successes and experiences. A good friend can be a wellspring of pleasure and joy, and those who live alone must make concerted efforts to maintain friendships with those who can best meet their needs.

People alone sometimes demonstrate a tendency to let friendships slide. The underlying reason may be a feeling of personal undesirability brought on by the feelings of rejection that often accompany a divorce or separation, or by the social stigma that is sometimes attached to being alone. Other times, not contacting friends can become a plain bad habit. Don't let it happen. Good friends are too hard to come by.

Take an aggressive role in maintaining your valuable friendships. Make it a point to call someone you haven't spoken to in a while or to invite a friend over or to go visiting. In this way not only do you maintain regular contact with friends, but you also create a weekly social opportunity or two.

Another way to ensure that vitally important human contact is maintained is in getting to know your neighbors. Be selective, of course, but take the time to get to know those that interest you. I have always had the good fortune to have marvelous neighbors. As my relationships with them have developed I have found that, with the combined support of friends and neighbors, I have little surrogate families all around me.

Supportive personal relationships can go a long way in helping you to combat your loneliness problem. That is why the wise selection and careful maintenance of such relationships remains one of the most important responsibilities you have to yourself as a person alone.

The Activites Aspect

In living alone, as one of my friends puts it, you have no one to "play with." If this is a problem for you, you may need to learn to have fun by yourself.

One of my psychology professors used to say, "You've got to have a little fun every day." For the person living alone and perhaps dealing with loneliness, this little bit of philosophy seems important.

Before I learned how to incorporate his advice into my life, I was always silently asking this professor, "How can I have fun when I am by myself?" As time went by, however, I made deliberate attempts to see if I could build a little fun into each day by engaging in some "solo" activities. I must confess thath the results of this simple experiment surprised me.

As an example, when I was first living alone there were times when I really wanted to go out for a nice steak dinner. However, dining out alone was pretty much considered taboo. After I had passed up several of those cravings for a steak, I began to consider going out to a nice restaurant on my own.

To be honest, it took a lot of courage, and when I walked in and requested a table for one, I felt a little awkward and self-conscious. But when the steak arrived at my table and I began savoring each bite, all of the awkwardness and feelings of trepidation melted away.

Not only had I broken a taboo, but I also had broken out of a self-imposed trap. This personal "breakthrough experience" was meaningful to me not only because it allowed me to make exciting dinner plans in the future, but, more important, because it freed me from the idea that I had to have the guaranteed companionship of another person before I could undertake such plans. Discovering that you can enjoy doing things and going places alone may open up a vast new territory of experience.

Learning to involve yourself in interests and activities that give you pleasure can be most rewarding. You may have to do some exploring, you may have to go through a few "breakthrough experiences," but when you succeed, you'll be glad you did.

What you do is not as important as just doing something. Do something you enjoy, undertake some physical activity, catch up on some reading, plan a future trip, go visiting, shopping or sunning. Bear in mind that a deliberate change of pace or scene can work wonders on feelings of loneliness.

Also know that by engaging in such activities you are not running away from yourself or your loneliness but are accepting the opportunity to enter into them solely in order to enhance your time alone. Your objective is not to escape but to add fulfillment to your life by providing yourself a variety of opportunities and experiences.

COMING TO TERMS WITH LONELINESS

The title of this chapter, "Combating Loneliness," implies that working through loneliness can sometimes be a battle. It is a battle you may not always win. You may sometimes feel crazy, desperate, afraid. But you can learn to live with loneliness, to overcome it and survive. Most important, in managing loneliness successfully you are able to remove the threat it poses to the single-living experience.

The ability to turn living alone into a satisfying experience depends to a great extent upon your ability to confront loneliness and to handle it in a positive, constructive way. If you avoid living alone purely because it has implications of loneliness, a significant opportunity for enhancing your dignity, maturity and personal growth can be missed.

The threat of loneliness is always there. It takes courage to accept it and to face it openly and honestly. It requires courage not to be afraid or overwhelmed by the fear of being alone.

Don't be afraid to experience your own loneliness. Strategies of escape can never replace the growth-inducing, deepening values that can come from winning your battle with loneliness. Gaining control over loneliness can give you strength and put you more fully in touch with your own resources.

At first the experience of loneliness can be frightening, even terrifying, but as you begin to make progress in combating it effectively, you will experience a new confidence.

The experience of loneliness may leave you feeling deprived at first, but once you have it under control it can lend new depth, awareness and meaning to your life. The battle against loneliness can be used as a springboard to personal growth. It can be a maturing experience.

In finally coming to terms with loneliness, bear in mind that the loneliness problem is really only amenable to a personal and private solution. There isn't anyone who can solve it for you. Other people can help, but they can't do the nitty-gritty work involved in breaking through the "loneliness barrier." That you must do.

4

Dealing with Aloneness

The concept of aloneness—of being by yourself in a purely physical sense—is welcomed by some who live alone. These individuals enjoy the peaceful state of tranquillity they find during the time they spend alone. Their moments of pure solitude are treasured, and, in some cases, jealously guarded. Many let it be known that they do not wish to have a potentially interfering other violate their quiet worlds.

On the reverse side of this almost blissful state of aloneness are those who see nothing positive in such an existence. For them, aloneness holds many possibilities —possibilities which generally manifest themselves in a single question: *How can I effectively compensate for the absence of another in my life?*

Unless positive answers are found to this query, unless ways are found to turn aloneness into a comfortable state of being, your potential for living alone and liking it will be greatly diminished.

COMPENSATING FOR THE ABSENCE OF ANOTHER

The inability to depend on companionship is a harsh fact in the lives of many loners. There is no one to make plans with, no one to come home to, no one with whom to share ideas and experiences. One must eat alone, sleep alone, and spend a lot of time alone.

The loner must assume total responsibility for everything from automobile maintenance to balancing the budget. It is not possible to enlist the aid of another in decision making or work sharing; nor may we look to another to provide financial support.

The lack of emotional closeness or the absence of an "intimate other" in the solo lifestyle is very troubling and painful to those who suffer from its effects. Because there is no one on the premises who cares and who can be cared for in return, many loners are left feeling empty. A woman who has lived alone for much of her life told me recently that, although she has adjusted well, she sorely misses the presence of another.

"Not to be held and loved and not to be able to give love to someone really hurts me inside at times. I think that the need for an ongoing, nurturing relationship is basic to human beings. We have to recognize that grown-ups need nurturing, too. I miss the touch and the warmth another can provide—sometimes just by being present. I have not found a way to compensate for it."

In essence, then, the person who lives alone lacks the constant physical presence of someone who can provide care, companionship, love and security. Very often there is no source of comfort when one is troubled or ailing or in need of help. For some this absence represents a huge void which must be filled by other means.

The key questions seem to be: How can I best get along without another? Can I develop ways and means of meeting my own needs in these areas, thereby minimizing some of the negative effects? Finally, are there effective ways to compensate for the absence of another in my life?

Rather than respond to these questions singularly, perhaps there is a collective kind of solution to them:

—*Develop self-responsibility*. The more responsibility you take for yourself and the quality of your life—the more you look not to others for strength and support, but to yourself—the less likely you will be to suffer from the absence of another.

—*Work hard to cultivate friendships and to strengthen family relationships*. Friends and family are the most important allies of the person who lives alone. Both are in a position to provide care and support. Involving them in your life regularly will help to minimize the negative effects of aloneness.

—*Do all you can to enhance your self-esteem.* Concentrate on presenting an attractive physical appearance, continuing to educate yourself, getting involved in worthwhile activities or endeavors. Those who hold themselves in high regard tend to have less need for others in their lives to help prop up a weak self-image.

—*Develop structured ways of dealing with aloneness.* Make plans in advance of what you know may be a lonely time. Vary your activities so that those which you do best alone are interspersed with those involving others. Plan a special occasion for yourself when you know you will be alone against your wishes. Careful planning can do much to reduce the negative impact of lonely periods.

—*Have someone you can always call on in times of trouble, physical injury or illness.* It can be a very calming, reassuring thing to know that there is another person who will provide care and support when you need it. Make special arrangements with an acquaintance, friend or neighbor to fill such a position.

It is unrealistic to assume that it is possible to compensate one hundred per cent for the absence of another in your life. Unless you are a completely happy hermit, there will be times when being alone is painful, no matter how well adjusted or well prepared you are.

Keeping the Blues out of "Together Times"

There are times when it just isn't fun to be alone—especially during mealtimes, holidays, weekends (particularly Saturday nights), and other times meant to be shared. These are the occasions when those affected must work the hardest to make being alone more an experience of living and less an experience of isolation.

HOLIDAYS

Holidays can produce moments of acute depression for the person alone. Even for people who live alone happily, holidays can be difficult. There is a feeling that "everyone's having a good time except me." I am happy to report, however, that this is changing.

In my family, holiday traditions carried their own special significance. Whether it was Mom's homemade doughnuts every Fourth of July or the sit-down dinners at Thanksgiving, these traditional touches seemed to enhance our enjoyment of being together. Once I'd left the nest, I found myself creating new approaches to the holidays by doing things which held special meaning for me.

Today, not only do these events give me something to center on and plan around, but it is so easy to include others. It has been rewarding to discover that other single people are developing customs of their own—a Christmas tree-trimming party, an Easter potluck, a Labor Day barbecue. New traditions are being established with friends, and holidays are no longer dreaded.

If, however, you are someone who suffers through the holidays regardless of circumstance, understand that the season will not last forever. You *can* make it through.

WEEKENDS

"Saturday night—the loneliest night of the week." I'm not sure how Saturday night received this tag, but it most likely was labeled by someone who, because he was alone, was excluded from the kinds of activities and celebrations usually associated with it.

The weekend, and Saturday night in particular, are definitely "together times" in our society, and I hold society partly to blame for the loner's special plight on these occasions. He is told that if he isn't doing something with other people on Saturday night, he *should* feel lonely.

I've talked with many loners who say that they manage very well every night of the week except Saturday. I'm always quick to assure them that if they can handle Tuesday or Wednesday, they can handle Saturday night as well.

Many of us become victims of a mind set which tells us that if we are supposed to be lonely, then we'd better act like it. So we sit around on Saturday nights and feel sad. Forget that it's Saturday, if you must! Pretend that it's a week night and pick up a good book or write a letter to a friend. Plan a special activity for yourself—a filet mignon dinner, perhaps.

If you are a gregarious person who enjoys being with others, make a deliberate attempt to break out of the patterns which might be restricting you. Invite people into your home—an entire party, if you like, or a friend for a TV-movie and popcorn. Get out and about and let others know that you are available for social events. You'll probably meet others who want to socialize, too. Don't be reluctant or allow pride to get in your way. Get out and mingle.

The most important thing for you to do is to keep working with yourself so that the weekends become comfortable times for you. One gentleman confessed to wearing himself out making the singles-bar scene before he was willing to consider staying home on a Saturday night.

"I can sit home alone on Saturday night and be happy with myself now," he told me. "I can read, watch television, have a drink alone and not be bothered by it. I actually enjoy myself more than I did going to bars, but I guess I needed the experience so I could appreciate my Saturday nights alone."

MEALTIMES

The subject of mealtimes is discussed in other sections of this book; it comes up here because so many people cite mealtimes as being among living alone's loneliest times. I understand what they mean from personal experience.

When I was living with my family, or dining in the college dormitory cafeteria, or sitting down to dinner with my roommates, the mealtime was always a sort of social occasion—a reason to come together, a time to "cuss and discuss" the day's events.

During my first year alone I noticed that a let-down feeling came over me whenever it was time to eat. Eventually food lost its appeal, except as a requisite for survival, and I became a pretty skinny kid. But, as I explain in other chapters, I found ways to deal with the problem, as you can if you follow some of these suggestions:

—*Do your best to make your meals alone appealing.* Purchase interesting foods. Experiment with new recipes. You may find that you enjoy your adventurous meals to such an extent that your mind will be taken off the fact that you're dining alone.

—*Read while you dine,* or do as many loners do, if you're so inclined: eat in the company of your television set.

Do whatever you can to help break the monotony of dining alone. Seek out dinner companions from time to time. Invite a friend to dinner. (You may receive an invitation in return.) Make arrangements to eat out with others from time to time.

My grandfather, a widower, long ago struck up a friendship with a lovely woman who lives in his apartment complex, and for more than fifteen years they have kept company at dinner time. They also enjoy the attendant pleasures of meal-planning, marketing and cooking together.

If you should have such an opportunity, by all means take advantage of it. If you must eat alone, work on preparing delectable, nutritious meals for yourself. More important, don't permit the absence of a dining companion to turn your mealtimes into miserable affairs.

Too many people alone allow themselves to develop poor eating habits when there is no one to cook for or dine with. This can lead to a state of deteriorating physical and mental health, but your nutrition is too important to your well-being for you to neglect it merely because you must eat alone most of the time.

SURVIVING THE LIVING-ALONE BLUES

In conversations with people who live alone, I've often come away with the distinct impression that many, in contending with their aloneness, consider themselves to be especially vulnerable to attacks of depression. They seem to feel that, because they are forced by the nature of their existence to dwell so much within themselves, they are more subject to these attacks than are those who are able to use the presence of others as an outlet and a counterbalancing force against them. I'm not sure that this is a valid assumption, but I know it is a very real feeling.

It is not uncommon, I suppose, for people in the beginning stages of living alone to be more vulnerable to depression than they might be once they have adjusted. If the depression is severe and the recovery lengthy, the memory may be painful and forever associated with the lifestyle.

Depression can cause people to view things unrealistically, and, unfortunately, a distorted perspective often has a way of perpetuating itself. Living alone can be perceived as a miserable sort of existence. For those caught in the throes of the "living-alone blues," the future looks bleak. Self-pity sets in. They sit and dwell on how they feel, which is rotten, and start to feel even worse. It becomes a vicious cycle. They feel confident they will be unable to overcome their depression.

The ability to adjust to living alone successfully depends to a great extent on one's ability to confront and to surmount inevitable periods of depression. Although most such cases of depression begin to disappear after a brief period of time, the crucial question for the person who succumbs to them as a direct or indirect result of living alone is: What can I do to minimize the occurrence of such unhappy periods?

The following strategies can be utilized by the person alone to help avoid the onset of depression in the first place.

—*Be aware that depression may occur as a result of living alone.* Awareness will help you gear up emotionally to handle it.

—*Become aware of the causes of your depression.* Learn to identify and do something to improve the root causes before the depression sets in.

—*Develop constructive, creative outlets.* This means doing anything which stimulates your thinking and allows you to concentrate on something outside yourself.

Involvement in an educational or cultural pursuit is one example.

—*Keep mentally and socially fit.* You don't need to be gregarious or have tons of friends, but you do need a basic, supportive social network.

—*Maintain some sort of work life or strong avocational involvement.* This sort of involvement ensures interest in life and can provide structure, security, and a feeling of belonging.

—*Take stock of your assets.* Let your mind dwell on them periodically. Just to be alive and healthy are two great blessings.

—*Accentuate positive thoughts and downplay negative ones.* Learn to view your situation from the standpoint of what you have going *for* you.

—*Cultivate your capacity for finding enjoyment in everyday life.* This means taking time to enjoy and appreciate a wide variety of sights, sounds and situations, such as the pleasures afforded by a spectacular sunset, by a brisk early-morning walk, by undertaking a hobby, or by planning things with family, friends and acquaintances. The more you are able to do this, the more you can reduce the likelihood of depression.

—*Greet each day with a purpose.* Form a "game plan" for the day. Have something definite planned and set out to accomplish it.

—*Look for adventure in life.* Be aggressive in your approach to living. Get involved in doing something exciting and constructive.

Should your most strenuous efforts to avoid depression fail, the following suggestions are designed to help you overcome any feelings of discouragement or apathy which may set in.

—*Be a self-starter.* Push toward what you know to be positive activity. Forcing activity is an excellent cure for depression.

—*Avoid boredom.* Boredom is a major component of depression. Routine boredom can be cured by seeking out new experiences.

—*Make a list of the things you like to do.* This is a good way to remind yourself that there are things that make you feel good.

—*Force yourself to be with people part of the time.* Too much time alone isn't good for anyone. Human companionship breaks monotony, creates balance and makes time spent alone easier to enjoy. Make it a point to establish regular contact with the outside world. There *are* other people out there. Many singles groups have parties and get-togethers. Many community groups are available which allow you to make human contact.

—*Reinforce your feelings of competence.*

Don't sit around and assume that you are helpless. Take part in hobbies, read interesting books, go to gyms or athletic clubs. Do anything that will help to improve your self-esteem.

—*Learn to pamper yourself.* We are generous in rewarding everyone except the one person who is most important to each of us—ourselves. The concept of pampering or rewarding oneself may seem contrived, but it can be an effective way of altering depression. Don't be stopped by the feeling that it somehow isn't right. Give yourself a present—something new to wear or a book to read. Purchase a luxury item—something you really want but have hesitated to buy for yourself. Living alone has its good points—like being able to spoil yourself! Indulge your whims!

—*Talk it out with a friend.* Unrestrained and honest emotional expression can relieve psychological pressures associated with depression and hasten recovery. Sometimes a talk with a good friend can mean the difference between regression and progression within a depressed state. Don't be afraid to confide. Suffering from depression is not a sign of weakness; it's part of being human.

—*Do something to help someone else.* Putting yourself in the service of others helps you to get outside yourself and takes your mind off your problems. Volunteers are needed for a number of charitable organizations. Not only will you be performing good services for others, but you will be getting your*self* out of the house and your *mind* off yourself.

—*Engage in some kind of physical activity.* The value of physical activity for reversing depression is well known. Exercise fills the senses with pleasure which in turn sends positive messages to the brain.

—*Plan for a change of scene.* Getting away from your immediate surroundings can work wonders as a mood elevator. A change of environment, though brief, can relax you and help to reorient your thinking.

—*Don't do anything that will make you feel worse.* For example, drinking alone is a not a good idea for a depressed person; listening to sad music or watching a sad movie will only compound a blue mood.

—*Seek help in the form of professional counseling.* If you feel that your situation is unbearable, professional counselors are acquainted with the depression syndrome and are prepared to help you make your way through it. Talk out your problems with people who can help rather than bottling up your frustrations.

There's Always a Way Out

During the years I've lived alone I've succumbed to many periods of depression—most of them the result of spending too much time alone. I did a lot of suffering until I learned to deal with my blue moods more effectively. I've used all of the aforementioned strategies singularly and in combination with good success.

In the beginning, I had a tendency to allow depression to roll over me and take me in its painful grasp. I became apathetic—at times immobile. I turned down invitations, avoiding the contact with people that I so desperately needed. During one of these depressed periods a friend refused to take "no" for an answer when he extended an invitation for a drive to the mountains. We hadn't been on the road five minutes when the depression began to lift. It taught me something.

On another occasion, when I had been living inside my own head to an extreme and was feeling too low to face the world, I called in sick at work, and then sat on the edge of my bed for an hour feeling miserable and not knowing what to do. Finally, in desperation, I picked up the phone and called my neighbor. Talking through the lump in my throat, I told her I needed help.

(This was significant for me because I had never been able to admit this kind of thing to anyone.) She invited me over and listened thoughtfully while I talked myself out. When I returned home I felt like a new person. Another lesson learned.

Diversions are never very difficult to find. If I am feeling depressed because of a need for companionship and am unable to contact anyone, I sometimes turn to my radio for company. One of the major networks in my area maintains around-the-clock talk-radio shows. When I tune them in, the people involved in the shows keep me company for hours. I don't feel lonely at all.

Over the years I have learned to recognize the symptoms of depression at their onset and have learned to reverse their effects before they take a toll. I simply tell myself, "You can either let your mood get the best of you, or you can do something about it." That "something" may be anything from restructuring my thinking along a more positive vein, to planning a deliberate change of scene, to jogging around the block. I find that when I fight depression, I usually win.

The important thing is to be aware that depression will set in occasionally. Knowing this, plan in advance what you will do when it strikes. True, the particular strategy one chooses will depend upon the nature or root cause of the depression. But do attempt to prepare yourself mentally in a way that will, as much as possible, serve to diminish the effects.

RIGIDITY: A HAZARD OF ALONENESS?

Rigidity is an ever-present potential hazard of living alone—a hazard which can come from not having to accommodate another in your day-to-day life. It is, however, something to which you may not have given much thought unless you, too, have fallen into the inflexibility trap.

I recall an incident in my high-school geometry class when a classmate tapped me on the shoulder and whispered a bit of gossip regarding our old-maid instructor. It was rumored around town that, after living alone for many years, she was so set in her ways that each night before she retired she went so far as to lay a single match next to the gas burner supporting her already prepared morning pot of coffee. *Wow*, I thought, I'd never go to that extreme. But then, I was never going to live alone, either.

Avoiding the Inflexibility Trap

Becoming rigid—set in your ways to the point of being inflexible—is an almost natural pitfall of the solitary lifestyle and one that I've engaged a long-standing personal battle against. With no one around to disrupt the order of your life or to cause you to vary your routines, it doesn't take long to get in the habit of doing things *your* way.

This may not be all bad, but I have found that it can cause problems for the loners, including myself, who fall into its trap. One can easily become unaccommodating to the extent that if something isn't done your way, it isn't done properly. This type of rigidity is unhealthy; it is tension-producing both for the perpetrator and for anyone who crosses his path. I can testify that it drives people away.

You wouldn't think that someone who was raised in a family of nine would grow into an inflexible adult, but it happened to me. Perhaps it was a natural backlash to having had to accommodate so many others for so many years during my youth. But I am more inclined to believe that rigidity is a part of my make-up which has been exacerbated by the fact that I live alone.

My war on inflexibility is a long way from being over. In the past few years, however, I have made a few small strides toward becoming a more adaptable person. From this vantage point I can name the strategies I have found to be most helpful in the hope that they will be of help to others:

—*Vary your routines as much as possi-*

ble. I once confessed to a professional psychologist that I was caught in a binding inflexibility trap and wished to find a way to conquer it. She recommended as a first step that I deliberately change the order in which I was accustomed to doing things during the first hour of every day. I was reluctant to do it but amazed at the results.

The thing it accomplished for me was to move the focus away from the importance of *order;* the object became merely to accomplish the same things—and in a more casual fashion. In some ways it was like playing a game. That in itself was relaxing and helped me to move away from rigidity.

—*Pinpoint the major contributing factor or factors to your inflexibility and take whatever steps are necessary to help you overcome it.*

I, for example, prefer a neat, orderly home environment. When I say neat and orderly, I don't mean casually clean. I mean white-glove perfection. I wasted a lot of time chasing half-full ashtrays, straightening pillows and dusting where there was no dust. I took a lot of kidding about vacuuming at midnight and was the recipient also of some not-so-nice comments.

I have always felt that the way my home looks reflects on me as a person. We all like nice reflections, but I carried it to an extreme. I would get the place fixed up just so, and because I was alone, it stayed that way. Let a guest come in and waterspot the marble vanity in the guest bathroom and I became a wreck until I could "undo the damage." A real case, right? The solution: I hired a housekeeper.

The focal point of the problem changed immediately, and what a relief it was! After the upkeep of the house became her responsibility, I no longer concerned myself with the little "damages" that she would be along to repair. Can't afford it, you say? I obviously couldn't afford not to. The housekeeper's wage represents the best money I've ever spent. I regard it as an investment in self-improvement.

This particular strategy has reduced my rigidity to a degree I did not believe was possible. I wish I'd done it much sooner.

—*Be around people all you can.* It is so easy for the person who lives alone literally to forget how to live with others. This is a great contributor to rigidity. Work at keeping yourself in an adaptable state by inviting guests to stay in your home from time to time. Be free to be a guest in someone else's home as well. Avoid developing hermitlike habits. Being with people can help keep you loose and flexible.

ALONENESS

Some who live alone tend to regard the lives of those who do not as being better or richer than their own. They envy those who do not have to contend with aloneness. Perhaps they would do well to consider that these people have not bought a perfect life in a jar labeled "togetherness." They must work with their togetherness just as you must work with your aloneness.

The discussion of dealing with aloneness does not end here. The succeeding chapters take you out into the world as a person alone, bring parts of the world into your world, and illustrate how effective management of your time alone can turn aloneness into a most comfortable state.

MAKING YOUR OWN FUN

5

Let Me Entertain You

In living alone you have no one with whom to keep constant company, so it becomes imperative that you learn to make your own fun, that you learn to entertain yourself and others without relying on the support of anyone else. Many people who live alone, especially those who are doing so for the first time, ask the same question: *How can I possibly plan anything that is fun, interesting or exciting when I don't have anyone to plan with?*

It seems that some people have perpetuated the idea that about the only thing a person alone can do to entertain himself is to engage in a lonely game of solitaire. Not true! Putting aside the old "it-takes-two" theme, you will be amazed at the number and quality of activities that do not require the presence of another person in order to be undertaken and to be ultimately pleasurable.

I have discovered over the years, both from personal experience and from observing others who live alone, that there are a multitude of ways to entertain yourself. Of course every individual is predisposed to certain types of activities, but the ideas and attitudes behind these undertakings are what we must examine here.

Although fun can be made and had in all sorts of ways, the person alone has a unique sort of problem to overcome: he has to rid himself of the old notion that fun can be had only in groups of two or more. The person who lives alone must assume a great deal of responsibility for making his own fun.

I held onto the "group-fun" myth for a long time myself—that is, until I began having experiences which taught me otherwise. I first discovered that it was fun to go window shopping alone. Then I began to enjoy browsing through a bookstore with no one to rush me. Later I found that going to a movie alone did not cause me to enjoy the movie less. The real surprises came on those occasions when I found that I had enjoyed myself doubly in the *absence* of a potentially interfering other.

The fact that I could take charge of and have control over the ways I chose to have fun became increasingly appealing. This is not to say that there weren't times when I thoroughly enjoyed the company of others, or when I knew that having a companion or two enhanced the pleasure or fun associated with a particular event. The point is simply that I could plan for and have fun on my own and make such experiences personally meaningful and edifying.

A PARTY FOR ONE?

Whoever heard of a party for one? I hadn't until one evening when I was all set to watch a movie on television and decided to make an occasion of it. I popped some popcorn, poured a frosty soft drink, sat back in my easy chair and enjoyed myself in a way that I never had before. The evening seemed somehow very complete.

When I began to analyze it, I came up with a curious but simple explanation for my added pleasure. Getting out the popcorn popper and pouring soft drinks were things I had always done for company, but never just for myself. When I gave *myself* this "special" treatment, I was surprisingly buoyed by the experience.

Since then I've made it a point to plan parties for myself from time to time. This may mean barbecuing hot dogs to go along with the World Series, fixing a cup of cappuccino for leisurely sipping in front of the fireplace, or buying and preparing all the ingredients for a gourmet dinner. I find that when I do these things, the resultant feelings of satisfaction and fulfillment linger on for days.

When I have recommended this type of self-entertainment to others who live alone, my suggestion has been met both with disdain and with curiosity. Some have told me outright that they thought it was an absurd idea. Others were intrigued but said that they could perceive it only as an experience that would emphasize their aloneness in a potentially negative way. To them, "party" applied strictly to a social gathering involving a number of people—never to a person alone.

For these Doubting Thomases I have a patented response: A party for one may be simple, it may be absurd, and it may hold the potential for being a lonely experience. What this sort of undertaking ultimately becomes depends on your attitude and approach to it. For me, a party for one has nothing but positive possibilities: It can lend an added dimension of pleasure to an otherwise routine activity (e.g., watching television); it can add a little spice to an otherwise uneventful evening; and, for me, it's an opportunity to be kind to myself and to have a little fun at the same time.

Aside from having your own private party, there are many other ways in which you, as a person alone, can make your own fun.

ENTERTAINING GUESTS

For many of us, inviting friends into our homes is an attractive and easy social alternative. Not only is the opportunity to entertain others present, but the opportunity to entertain ourselves in the process exists also. Two birds with one stone. A double bonus.

But the idea of entertaining guests is a common trouble spot for some who live alone. These individuals claim that feelings of inadequacy and helplessness often surface at such times. At the same time, however, many marvelous hosts and hostesses are persons who entertain unassisted. What accounts for this disparity?

I can think of three specific areas which singularly or collectively may have bearing, and these are: (1) the suitability of a given individual's personality to entertaining, (2) the type of environment to be used for entertaining, and (3) the reservations some people may feel about hosting or hostessing without benefit of partner.

No doubt your personality has a great deal to do with whether or not you choose to entertain. Some people just have more flair for entertaining than others. There is a retired divorcée living near me who does more entertaining than anyone I know.

Friends seem to come and go from her place in a steady stream. I often see a huge stew kettle sitting outside her front door, waiting to be hosed out following an evening get-together. Whenever I smell the wonderful aroma of her spaghetti sauce wafting across the way, I know that later I will hear the sounds of people enjoying themselves. And I always do.

Some who live alone just do not consider themselves entertaining types; they prefer to wait for invitations rather than issue them. This is certainly to be respected; however I would caution such people: Don't miss out on this easy opportunity to socialize, and don't feel that you are obligated to "perform" once guests have arrived. The object is simple: to enjoy one another's company.

The second consideration—the type of environment to be used in entertaining—is a problem for some people. For example, a person who once invited guests into a spacious home may not feel that a smal apartment lends itself well to entertaining. Others may feel obliged to apologize for what they feel are inadequate furnishings or surroundings. As a rule, however, few people are as critical of the way another person lives as is the person himself; guests are just pleased to be invited.

The logistics of hosting a gathering alone can present real problems to you if you're new at it. I am reminded here of a conversation I had with a forty-year-old executive who lived in an elegant townhouse. He was reluctant to invite guests, even though he was eager to share his new surroundings. He wondered how he could possibly entertain properly when he had to be in two places at once—the kitchen and the living room.

As we talked it over, I encouraged him to move freely between the two rooms. Guests are capable of entertaining one another, and he wasn't going to be expected to perform a juggling act while the soufflé burned.

Some who live alone make it a practice to invite a friend to act as cohost or hostess when they entertain. This helps to relieve the pressure of being a single host. The need for a cohost or hostess may be determined by the size and type of party which you plan to give. In any case, it is a matter of preference.

This brings us to another point of exploration for the person alone who wishes to entertain. What kinds of things can you do to entertain guests successfully?

The Dinner Party

Many people feel that having company for dinner demands expensive food and fancy dishes. This simply isn't true. The person who has accepted an invitation to dinner in someone else's home is usually in a positive and receptive mood to begin with. You don't have to be a gourmet cook or even know how to boil water to entertain successfully at mealtime. One of the "meals" I most enjoy serving my guests consists of three simple ingredients: sourdough bread, sliced cheese, and fresh fruit. This is known as a "peasant's dinner," but when a nice wine or chilled champagne is added, no one feels impoverished.

Keep in mind that people love to be invited. They come without grand expectations, happy to have an evening away from their own surroundings.

Another popular type of informal gathering is the Potluck Dinner. Very simply, for the Potluck Dinner each guest brings a dish to the home of the host or hostess. Sometimes the type of dish to be brought is designated by the host to ensure a balanced meal; on other occasions guests are asked to bring their specialty dishes for others to sample.

A variation of the Potluck is commonly known as the "BYO," or "Bring Your Own." An example of this type of dinner party is one for which the host or hostess prepares a salad and baked potatoes and asks each guest to bring his or her own steak.

An extreme example of this kind of party occurs when each guest is asked to bring a favorite "fast-food" meal to someone's home. The congregation consumes together, the emphasis being more on the company than on the food.

The obvious advantage of the Potluck and BYO dinners for the person alone is that they are easy to host, thus removing the pressure some may feel when they want to entertain.

Some who live alone delight in preparing and giving a completely formal dinner party with everything from roast duckling to crystal wine goblets and linen napkins. Preparations may take a full day or more, but for them that is part of the fun.

Regardless of the type of dinner party, the objective for the person alone is to create an opportunity for socializing. There are other popular ways in which singles entertain without a lot of fuss and bother. Let's take a look at some of them.

The After-Dinner Get-Together

One of the easiest ways to entertain, especially for those who feel uncomfortable about having guests at mealtime, is to invite friends for an after-dinner party. Nothing is required of the host or hostess except hospitality. Very often dessert and coffee are served, or perhaps an after-dinner drink or glass of wine.

I know of one fellow who enjoys entertaining this way in the evenings. He stops off at a local bakery on his way home from work, picks up a fresh French pastry or savory strudel and, later on, brews some espresso. His friends look forward to his invitations.

The Wine-and-Cheese Social

Another easy-to-host social function is the wine-and-cheese party. This party requires nothing more of the host than that he issue invitations to friends to bring bottles of wine and their favorite cheeses. All bottles are opened and cheeses sliced for sampling. The host may provide crackers, if he chooses, to clear the guests' palates as they sample. For the person alone this kind of party pretty well takes care of itself.

The "Special-Event" Party

Some people prefer to center a party or get-together around certain special events. In many cases the special occasion is not the typical birthday or anniversary celebration, but is connected with a popular media event, like the Super Bowl, the Academy Awards presentation, or a championship fight. The obvious advantage, of course, is that the television acts as a sort of cohost, freeing the host or hostess to attend to all hospitality requirements.

The Game Plan

I have a single friend who hosts frequent "game nights" in her home. When the guests arrive, each has the option of engaging in all sorts of games—everything from cards to charades. Very often a new game comes on the scene and everyone's attention is focused on it for an evening. The advantage of this type of gathering, again, is that a whole evening's entertainment is built into it.

GO AHEAD; IT'S GOOD FOR YOU

Before we move on to other ways in which you can make your own fun, a final word on entertaining guests: there need be nothing complex or demanding about it. Maintaining social contact with others is necessary to our mental well-being, and there is little in that realm to equal good company and good conversation. Most people appreciate invitations and are only too glad to accept; someone's home is a very nice place to be invited into.

6

Hobbies and Pastimes

When a person retires, his doctor often will recommend that he take up a hobby or develop an interest that will give his life balance and enrichment. Satisfying hobbies and pastimes have been known to increase longevity because of the stimulation and sustaining type of involvement they can provide.

For the individual who is living alone, having a hobby or pastime is no less important. Such undertakings assume significance in that the person alone often has a great deal of free time which he or she has to manage. A worthwhile hobby or pastime can offer endless hours of pleasure, enjoyment and satisfaction.

Because the myriad types of hobbies and pastimes are too numerous to list and because undertaking one or the other is a personal, individual kind of thing, I do not wish to get into prescribing either. However, I do hope to portray, through example, certain kinds of hobbies and pastimes in order to stimulate the reader's thinking and to illustrate the value of such undertakings in the lives of persons who live alone.

The first example which comes to mind involves a 42-year-old computer systems analyst who, in living alone for the first time, began to decorate and fill an empty apartment with various kinds of plants. Before he knew it, he was studying books on plant care, building terrariums, and advising others in his apartment complex on the care and feeding of their plants.

He expressed his surprise and pleasure at the joys associated with his newly cultivated hobby: "The irony of the whole thing really stuns me. When I was living with my wife, we had plants in the house, but since she cared for them, I never really paid them much attention. When I moved into this apartment, however, I found that it felt empty and cold. After I brought a couple of plants home from the supermarket, the place really seemed to warm up.

"I gradually learned to care for them and became a 'green thumb' of sorts. I grew to enjoy visiting nurseries and learning about all kinds of indoor and outdoor plants. Right now I have more than twenty different types, and tending to them takes a lot of time. I enjoy every minute, though. I find it a very constructive way to spend my time."

This gentleman stumbled onto a pastime

which later became a hobby. Very often a hobby isn't something one plans for, but is an evolving kind of thing resulting from another experience. I remember the spring I decided to grow patio tomatoes in containers on my front porch. I was following the example of a friend whose delicious wares I had consumed the summer before. Until that time I hadn't known it was possible to raise homegrown tomatoes outside of a backyard garden.

I can't tell you how many hours of pleasure and good eating those tomatoes provided. From the time I brought the baby plants home, transferred them to one-gallon, corrugated containers, fed them, watered them, and watched the blossoms, then tomatoes, appear, I was totally engrossed in a very rewarding pastime.

Gardening, whether indoor or outdoor, affords many people hours of enjoyment. Even those who have never had a prior interest have found it to be engrossing and fun. One of my friends has cultivated an extensive herb garden in the windowsills of her kitchen. She snips them for use in preparing gourmet soups and other succulent dishes.

My grandfather, a widower now in his eighties, used to spend hour upon hour tending prize rosebushes in his backyard. He knew more about the growing of a perfect rose than any man I knew, and it was a hobby that helped to fill a void after my grandmother passed on.

Hobbies and pastimes do play an important part in filling the voids in the lives of individuals new to living alone. I am reminded of two widowed acquaintances who lost their husbands within months of one another and who were having an understandably difficult time filling the interminable hours that had once been devoted to their mates.

During one of our "learning-to-live-alone" discussions, I suggested the possibility of getting into rug hooking as a simple activity which required no expertise but which would help them fill their time constructively until they had passed through the difficult reorientation stage. In the end, I suggested, they would have something to show for the time spent, and, in the meanwhile, their minds would be occupied and their hands busy.

I recall how reluctantly they went through the catalog—neither being interested by or in much of anything—but each ordered a rug, one to fit the decor of her home and the other to make as a gift. When the rugs arrived, both ladies got right to work and were quickly caught up in the infectiousness of their individual projects. Before long they were "hooking" together on evenings and weekends and became known to themselves and to me as the "Happy Hookers." They did seem happier, too.

Not long ago I visited the home of an electrical engineer and was surprised to see what I immediately recognized as a custom-made rug in front of his fireplace. When I inquired about it, he told me this story:

"After my divorce, I raced around frantically to all of the local night spots. I just couldn't sit at home. After a while, though, when I became tired of the nightly rat race, a friend suggested I try hooking a rug as he had done. The next thing I knew, I was enjoying my evenings at home working on my rug. It was so much fun to watch the darn thing take shape that I couldn't leave it alone. Let me tell you, it was a relaxing, rewarding change from chasing all over town. It really helped me settle down. Now I feel I have something to stay home for. It may sound silly, but I'm 'hooked'—as soon as I finished it, I started another."

He then took me to his den and showed me an intricately designed five-by-eight-foot masterpiece-in-progress.

Naturally, rug hooking isn't for everyone. Some might find it dull or boring. I am one of those people who can't sit idle, so I enjoy rug hooking when I am too washed out to do anything else, but want to do something productive.

Another activity which is enjoyed by many who live alone is working jigsaw puzzles. A thirty-year-old bachelor explains how he became engrossed in them as a pastime which later developed into a hobby:

"At first I got into it for something to do. I had enjoyed puzzles as a kid and decided to try my hand at it as an adult. I love to get involved with jigsaws that have a 'jillion' pieces. Recently I did a couple of country scenes that were too nice to take apart, so I turned them over, painted the backs with glue, and applied a light shellac to the front. Then I framed them and hung them as pictures. I plan to mount the next one on an end table in my den."

His story brought back the memory of a time when, in the early stages of living alone, I was having a particularly difficult battle with a case of depression brought on by loneliness. Absolutely nothing appealed to me. The spell lingered for days and I did a lot of sitting and staring and grieving. Just by chance I got involved in putting a jigsaw puzzle together, and within a matter of hours I discovered that I had snapped out of the depression and into some fresh, positive thinking.

That experience taught me something about the value of a constructive, mind-occupying activity for the person who may not have the presence of other people to assist him in working through his depression or loneliness. Do *anything*, but don't just sit.

Reading is a pastime which provides escape, enlightenment, amusement and adventure to many people. Aside from being a worthwhile, mind-occupying activity, the nicest thing about reading is that it is an activity which can be pursued on a totally individualized basis. And the market of reading materials is so broad that something exists for almost everyone—from the uninterested to the mildly interested to the avid reader. It's just a matter of doing a little exploring until you find something that appeals to you.

A book, a magazine, or a newspaper article can open new doors for the reader. Recently I was rather absent-mindedly browsing through my monthly automobile-club magazine when I stumbled upon an article that outlined a complete "trip for one" to a Western ski resort during the off-season. Entitled "Sun Valley Summer," the story was an invitation to enjoy the beauties of the resort and the surrounding countryside at a time other than peak season. The article and accompanying pictures held so much appeal for me that I am planning to make the trip. When I consider that the idea would never have occurred to me otherwise, I am very glad for having picked up that magazine.

Because of my strong belief in the value of reading as a worthwhile and stimulating pastime, I recommend to all who live alone that they subscribe to a daily newspaper. Somehow the routine arrival of current printed material gives the person alone something to depend on, and, once delivered, a newspaper can provide all kinds of entertainment—from the editorials to the sports pages to the crossword puzzle.

When I was first living alone in a community where I knew no one, I could count on the newspaper to arrive every evening like a good friend. For me it was a form of contact with the outside world, and reading it after dinner became a pleasurable nightly ritual which I enjoy to this day.

I believe also that magazine subscriptions have an important place in the life of the person who lives alone. I know a fellow who couldn't seem to get both feet on the ground after his wife left. For a time his whole life seemed to stop. When he began to assume an active role again, he seemed to take a tentative approach to even the simplest commitments.

In an attempt to help him settle into a more productive and satisfying living routine, and to bring some new things into his life, I suggested that he subscribe to a daily paper as well as a couple of weekly magazines. His attitude was fairly negative toward the idea. He felt that those things no longer had value for him. In his mind, a husband and wife shared a newspaper at the breakfast table, but a person alone had no use for one.

It took a lot of convincing. His stubborn refusal made me all the more determined to prove my point, so I gave him a gift subscription to a national weekly news magazine. When he confessed his pleasure at the arrival of each edition, that was thanks enough for me. He later told me that as reading each issue became a part of his living routine, he began to enjoy his time at home more on the days when the latest edition arrived. And not long after that he began stopping off at a newsstand on the way home from work to pick up a paper.

Between the newspapers and magazines, his life began to take on a more positive and meaningful structure. This was an interesting turning point for him in that he became less inclined to stay away from home and less dependent on others to entertain him than he had been during the months following his separation.

Reading is a means by which the person alone can communicate with himself and the world. It can serve to rechannel negative thinking. Books can become companions of sorts. The more reading material the person alone can bring into his life, the less likly he is to suffer from one of the common maladies attributed to living alone: too much time and too little to do with it.

Simplistic, you say? Perhaps so. However, if there is anything a person can do to help himself spend time alone constructively, I'm for it.

There is no end to the number and types of hobbies and pastimes we could explore in this chapter, but listing them and discussing them individually really is not the point. Perhaps this story makes the point best.

Caroline J. is a single woman in her mid-thirties who confesses that she spent many years doing "a lot of nothing," waiting for the day she would marry. As time went by and that day never came, she found herself mired in a deep rut. Her days consisted only of activities related to survival: eating, working and sleeping.

In her words, "It was a pretty dull and dangerous existence. I was eating myself alive with my own thoughts. I really needed a way to get outside myself. About the time that I was ready to devour myself totally, a friend got me interested in oil painting. One thing led to another: First it was a stimulating pastime; later it developed into a fullblown hobby and finally became an avocation of sorts. I am now a member of an amateur artists guild, and we arrange our art shows in shopping centers on the weekends. I don't want to remember my life before I became involved in art. I can't believe that I allowed myself to live that way."

Because for many single people there is a great deal of free time to manage, time which in many cases had been relegated to others, it is only wise to develop personally enriching ways to spend that time. People alone, with little extra activity to fill their time constructively, too often fall into a pattern of dwelling solely on themselves. This trap can turn into a vicious cycle of brooding, self-pity, self-degradation, and little, if any, personal productivity.

Too much living with oneself is not good. A mentally healthy, well-balanced person must have creative outlets for himself and his thoughts. A well-chosen hobby or pastime offers, in very simple, accessible ways, just such an outlet.

7

Stepping Out the Door

"The man who goes alone can start today; but he who travels with another must wait till that other is ready."

—*HENRY DAVID THOREAU*

For some who live alone, particularly those who have never married, going out alone is the easiest, most natural thing in the world, while for others, especially those who are new to being on their own, it is one of the most difficult and disheartening prospects with which they are faced.

In stepping out the door the person alone ventures into a predominately paired world. It can be awkward and embarrassing at times and can make one feel especially self-conscious. On the other hand, venturing out alone offers the chance to explore and experience situations and people in a totally open and unrestricted fashion. The opportunities for fun and adventure are unlimited.

After many years of going places on my own, I've concluded that it comes down to a simple question of attitude. True, it does take a succession of such experiences to build your confidence and to develop in you a positive attitude, but successful solo ventures can be accomplished with a minimum of personal discomfort and conflict, even in the beginning. All that is required in any given situation is that you present yourself as a total, "together" human being, capable of enjoying yourself whatever the circumstances.

Sometimes, especially in the beginning, you may have to hide behind a display of false confidence. However, projecting an open, straightforward attitude, without apologizing verbally or nonverbally for the fact that you are alone, goes a long way in assuring acceptance from others. An apologetic look or stance on the part of an adventuresome loner can be an automatic turn-off to would-be companions.

One of the most destructive things a loner can do is to relegate himself to reclusion because of a fear of stepping out the door alone. This is not to say that such a fear may not be well-founded, but rather that it must be overcome, as any other fear must be. Stepping out the door alone can be likened to jumping into a swimming pool when you know that the water is cold. Immersing one pinkie at a time only prolongs the agony. It's wiser just to plunge in. And the sooner you do it, the better!

GOING PLACES ALONE

Except for those few social exercises which may require an escort, I cannot think of a place or event that cannot be visited or attended by a person alone. But before we get to the places and events, let's take a look at some of the advantages in going out alone.

The most obvious advantage, of course, is in being able to come and go as you please. Have you ever longed to leave a party, a bad movie, or some other unpleasant event, only to have to wait until your social partner was ready? Not so when you are alone. You can take complete charge of your comings and goings. I find this an especially rewarding aspect of freedom.

Another advantage of going out alone is that it allows room for true spontaneity. Because you are alone, it is not necessary for you to make plans ahead of time or to secure permission from anyone. Your adventure potential is increased by the fact that you are free to go at a moment's notice. You can, in effect, become an actual "free spirit."

How many times have you had to ignore your own interests or do something you didn't want to do in order to keep harmony with another? When you live alone, you are completely free to pursue your own outside interests. No more getting coerced into giving up begrudged hours to indulge someone else's whims.

Dining Out Alone

Dining out alone seems to cause more consternation among those who live alone than any other outside activity. My personal experience in this area was discussed in an earlier chapter, but it might be beneficial here to mention a few considerations.

In the first place, I would hate to see anyone give up this potentially pleasurable experience just because he or she lacks a dining partner. Although you may feel slightly awkward or conspicuous in the beginning, these feelings will diminish as your experiences with dining out alone increase. Whatever you do, don't cross it off your agenda without at least having given it a few tries.

I think that the restaurant and the hour at which you choose to dine are important considerations. Some restaurants—generally the smaller, quainter places—are more conducive to the single diner than others. Become familiar with those in your area. You may want to try dining early, before the crowds arrive. This will allow you to dine in relaxed fashion, especially if occupying a table meant for two or more makes you feel uneasy.

Some diners get in the habit of carrying reading material with them when they visit a restaurant. For some it provides "company" and helps them relax when they dine; others frankly admit that they like having something to "hide behind." Whatever the reason, if it's something you prefer to do, then by all means do it!

Meeting People

I have no compunctions about attending the theater, a movie, a sporting event or any other outside activity by myself. Such events may or may not be more enjoyable with a companion, but I never let the fact that I am alone stop me. If it's something I want to see or do, I go.

One of the biggest advantages in going out alone is that you are afforded the opportunity to meet other people without restrictions. In my own experience, the people I have met have been very receptive toward me as a person alone. If they happen to be alone themselves, they often are eager to communicate. And most couples I meet, rather than being threatened by or uncomfortable about the fact that I am alone, seem to take an almost protective attitude and go out of their way to ensure that I have a good time.

Few human beings enjoy isolation. That's why I urge you, if you live alone, to go out and talk to others, not just to people you know, but to strangers—especially to strangers. If you are afraid of other people or afraid of rejection, the quickest cure is to get out and make contact deliberately. The more you do it, the more you'll enjoy it. (This comes from one who has overcome a painful case of shyness and who, in the process, has met many friendly people.)

Okay, you may ask, where do I start?

—Start by learning to take the initiative. If you always leave it to others to assume the assertive role, you're going to miss out on a lot.

—Learn the art of being "meetable." Be open; let a friendly smile ease you into introductions and conversations. Show genuine concern for others in a way that lets them know you are aware of their uniqueness as human beings; in other words, be interested—not interesting. Too many people think that to be "appealing" they must become dynamic, fascinating individuals—people too interesting for anyone to resist. The fact is, most people are drawn to a person who shows genuine interest in *them*.

—Don't hesitate to strike up a conversation anywhere you choose. It does seem that people today, as a rule, seldom wear very receptive expressions. However, behind those stoic masks are a lot of friendly people waiting to be unmasked by another friendly person. Why shouldn't it be you?

Okay, you may ask, what do I say? The answer is simple: whatever comes naturally. People are quick to spot contrived questions and statements and will often react by turning a cold shoulder. Make whatever you say as naturally representative of you or the situation as you can. People are quick to spot genuineness, also, and will almost always respond favorably and receptively.

Sometimes even the contrived introduction works, provided you use it correctly. Say for example that you approach a fellow passenger on the deck of an ocean liner and ask, "Pardon me, but do you live around here?" It may be awfully corny, but it can't be said you aren't trying. At the very least you will have done your part in breaking the ice.

Adventures Great and Small

When the person alone steps out the door, there is no limit to the types of adventures that await him or her. The rationale behind undertaking any kind of adventure, be it great or small, is that a change of scene can be fun, restful and relaxing. Also, since the loner has no one with whom to interact on a constant basis, it really behooves him or her to get out and mix often.

One of the easiest things a person alone can do is to go for a walk or take a drive. Although it might seem to some like a lonely undertaking at first, a walk or drive can be refreshing. Engaging in either can help shake off the doldrums and stimulate positive thinking.

During the years I have lived alone, I've frequently felt sort of "logjammed" —in a rut. Having no one around with whom to exchange ideas, those ruts have sometimes grown pretty deep. Although it may go against what I feel like doing at the time, getting out for a walk, a drive or some other activity has never failed to reduce or eliminate feelings of mental entrapment.

One summer I took on the responsibility of caring for a friend's luxury automobile while she was away. The car had a tape player and an exquisite stereo system. I quickly became addicted to going for drives with a favorite cassette to keep me company. I can still recall the feeling I had of being recharged after each drive. I was very reluctant to return that source of pleasure to its rightful owner at the end of the summer.

Another of my favorite small adventures is getting out and searching the specialty shops for the best of everything—the finest baked goods, the best produce, the most enticing gourmet imports. It has become a form of entertainment which I thoroughly enjoy. Specialty shops offer a relaxing sort of ambience and an opportunity to enlarge one's tastes.

Some loners may feel that specialty items are out of their price range, and they may be in some cases. However, I have developed a rationale which makes them seem affordable to me: they become part of my entertainment at a pittance of the usual entertainment expense. This puts their cost in a different perspective. I can bring home a choice filet mignon, for example, at one-third the cost of dining out; a really fine bottle of wine can be purchased for the same price as two or three drinks in a pub. The examples are endless and often the fruits of a simple adventure can be savored over a longer period of time than just an evening—as in the case of, say, a small brick of gourmet cheese or a bag of specially mixed ground coffee. This is also an excellent way for the person alone to "treat" himself!

Another of my favorite pursuits as a person alone is the purchase of season tickets to a local playhouse, theater or sporting event. There was a time when I would never have considered such a thing. I regarded attendance at such an event as purely a "couple" undertaking.

Through the rather forceful insistence of

a friend who understood the values inherent in this kind of enterprise, I purchased a season ticket to summer softball. While it is impossible to recount all the positive experiences that came about as a result of that decision, perhaps the most outstanding was the chance to meet people who shared the same interest. The feeling of camaraderie—almost a sense of family—that came from being with the same people over a period of time, while sharing a common passion, made for a very rewarding adventure. All in all, it turned out to be one of the most enjoyable experiences of my life.

Some of the potentially great adventures for the person alone come under the realm of travel. Unfortunately, many loners are reluctant to travel by themselves. While this reluctance can be understood, it would seem a shame to miss out on a chance to visit new places out of fear.

Until they've done it, many loners express dread at the idea of traveling alone. Most seem to avoid it because of feelings of awkwardness or insecurity or lack of guaranteed companionship. Just like so many other experiences you can have alone, once you've taken a trip on your own, you may very likely ask yourself why you didn't do it sooner.

There is no doubt that the prospect of traveling alone initially may require a bit of courage. Fortunately, however, you need not take on the planning of a trip alone. A travel agent can be a real ally in making you feel more secure about many of the trip details such as tickets, transportation and lodging. A good agent will provide you with plenty of literature about the place you plan to visit. Getting acquainted with such things as customs, climate, and necessary attire will help to enhance your feelings of security.

The most popular types of trips for all but the most independent are generally cruises and tours—the obvious advantage, of course, being that there are many other people who also are traveling alone. Both offer self-contained, all-inclusive travel packages which have appeal for a traveler who may feel somewhat insecure.

An elderly friend of mine, who for years had expressed tremendous misgivings about traveling alone, took an interesting plunge into solo travel one recent summer. She had learned from an acquaintance that it was possible in July and August to stay on certain college campuses as a guest at modest cost. Before she thought twice about it, she was booked into a residence hall on a New England campus for one week.

She reveled in the experience. The structured environment had particular appeal for her and completely quelled her fears about traveling by herself. She was delivered to the dormitory, given a room, and for the rest of the week enjoyed the recreational facilities and cultural opportunities at the school. All her meals were provided in the dormitory cafeteria, eliminating the need to search alone for places to dine in an unfamiliar town. "I've never been anywhere where people were so friendly," she told me, "and I'm going back again."

Some of the more independent loners enjoy traveling alone so much that they wouldn't have it any other way. A single traveler has a way of attracting people which opens the door for companionship and broadens the opportunity for fun and adventure.

If you are insecure about traveling alone, it is a good idea to experiment with short trips in the beginning. Then, when you get your sea legs, you will perhaps be ready to take an extended trip on your own.

When stepping out the door into simple or great adventures, the person alone can open new vistas at every turn, whether viewing the newest museum display, taking a trip across the Atlantic, or attending opening night at the local playhouse. Take the initiative; it's all yours. And the fun is all yours, too.

EXPANDING YOUR SOCIAL NETWORK

Beyond entertaining guests and getting out and meeting people, there are other ways in which the single person can significantly expand his or her social network. One of the most common ways of doing this involves stepping out the door into established social environments such as colleges, churches, volunteer organizations, clubs and various interest groups. Here are places to meet potential companions and make new friends. Let's explore some of the advantages.

Continuing Education

Opportunities abound as never before in community colleges and universities. Course offerings range from Arabic to Zen; they include classes on adult fitness, dryland skiing, classic cars, the building of greenhouses, handwriting analysis, gourmet cooking, and real-estate marketing, to name only a few. I counted over five hundred different courses in one catalog alone. New York University's continuing education program offers more than eight hundred selections.

Colleges are madly recruiting the older, more serious students, and these students are enrolling in droves. California's community-college system catered to a staggering 1,265,000 adults in 1976—one out of every eight adults in the state.

Contemporary weekend seminars are becoming an extremely popular way to learn and socialize at the same time. Recently a course entitled "Getting Along Alone" attracted an enormous crowd on one campus of the University of California. Films and lecture series are also drawing well.

This boom in adult courses can open new areas of exploration for the person living alone. A good class can provide an outlet as well as a chance for adventure. The following course descriptions, taken from a University of California continuing education catalog, are examples of the variety of experiences currently offered:

> YOSEMITE IN WINTER . . . three full days of hiking, snow-shoeing and cross-country skiing in Yosemite National Park.

If you're an outdoorsman, you merely have to show up! All the planning has been done for you.

Or how about this one:

> CHARLESTON, SAVANNAH, NEW ORLEANS . . . Visit beautifully preserved Colonial and Ante Bellum homes and plantations . . . world famous gardens . . . Tour New Orleans French Quarter, the View Carre, its famous antique shops and historic monuments, Jackson Square, Pirate's Alley, St. Louis Cathedral . . . hear Dixieland Jazz at Preservation Hall . . . take guided tours of art museums . . . visit

private homes, city markets, Charleston's Cabbage Row... Daily luncheons featuring Southern and French-Creole specialties.

Wow! Who wouldn't like to go? Keep in mind that these are only two of many types of classes. I think it must be difficult to browse through one of these catalogs and not find something of interest and appeal. In most community-college systems classes are offered free of charge, while at state colleges and universities fees are required —some nominal and others more expensive.

A growing number of people are spending summer vacations on college and university campuses, studying everything from ceramics to constitutional law in special low-cost programs combining leisure with learning. The vacation colleges are usually sponsored by alumni associations, but most are open to non-alumni as well. There are no prior educational requirements and the programs do not carry credits toward a degree.

Prices vary, but a week or ten-day program for one, including room, board and tuition, usually runs between $200 and $300. Participants attend cultural, recreational and educational activities on the campus and are free to go sight-seeing off the campus if they choose.

Interest in this kind of vacation is growing for several reasons. Many people seem more interested in learning for its own sake than in accruing credits, and there is a certain appeal in returning to, or just being on, a college campus. Some find being able to combine vacation with travel and study very attractive.

Whatever the reason, it impresses me as being a novel way for the person alone to expand his social network. A college campus can be an ideal setting for meeting other people. Common types are generally drawn together to pursue common interests, and this establishes grounds for a potentially rewarding sort of social rapport.

Some people, especially those who have been away for a while, may feel a little hesitant toward returning to school. If this applies to you, keep the following in mind. A return to school does not have to be related to job or career prospects; classes are offered in many fields of interest, including practical living and personal growth and enrichment. Do not let age or other concerns of dubious validity deter you. Do all the exploring you can. Opportunities abound for real personal growth. If your experience turns out in any way like mine —well, school has never been so much fun!

Clubs and Special-Interest Groups

For the individual alone who finds it difficult to make new social contacts, as well as for the person who enjoys getting out and doing with someone else whatever he or she likes to do, clubs and special-interest groups can be a lot of fun.

There are literally hundreds of groups one can join—everything from the Beer Can Collectors of America to the Singles Outings Club, from the International Frisbee Association to the Procrastinators' Club of America; there's a group for every taste. A listing of those in a particular area appears in the phone directory yellow pages under Clubs, Associations, Fellowships and the like. Also, many are listed weekly in the local newspaper's "clubs and activities" calendar. So many possibilities exist that I find it delightfully mind-boggling. Clubs and interest groups not only are great places for creating new social relationships, they offer the added advantage of ongoing involvement as well.

Church Groups

Some find church-sponsored groups easy to join. Meeting other people in a comparatively protected environment offers advantages to those who may feel insecure about expanding their social networks in other ways. Many church groups extend their social activities through the weeknights and weekends, providing continuing social contact for the members. One nondenominational church with which I am familiar sponsors a mountain retreat for its members and schedules weekend and summer outings throughout the year. If this has appeal for you it might be worthwhile to investigate those in your area.

Volunteer Organizations

Some who are alone prefer to put themselves in the service of others as a means of expanding their social contacts. For them it is an especially worthwhile endeavor in that they are able to help others at the same time that they are helping themselves.

Investigating volunteer opportunities in a particular area might be the beginning of a new lease on life for the person living alone who is devoid of opportunities for regular contact with people. Somehow, helping others has a way of making one's life more meaningful, and getting involved in volunteer work is very easy. Often it requires no more than the offering of one's time.

If you are interested but don't know where to begin, identifying your interests and talents can help give direction. There are numerous possibilities in the area of charity work, hospital work, and public-school work, to name a few. The following excerpt was taken from a newspaper ad seeking volunteers in several areas:

> A specialist is needed to evaluate and price antique dolls and rare books for sale...volunteers are needed to sort jewelry and repair bicycles, provide carpentry help, tutor an 18-year-old automobile accident victim....

Opportunities such as these exist in abundance everywhere. The interested individual need only investigate them.

THE IMPORTANCE OF GETTING OUT

Leading a well-balanced life is a primary objective for the person living alone. One way to meet this objective is to develop the ability to make positive human contact. Such contact can be made in many ways. The initiative lies with you. Investigate hobby groups, social-interest groups, or educational ventures. You may have interests that you've not yet developed in your life. As a person alone you are free to do whatever you want to do. *This is a time for exploration.*

In order to assume new social roles, you must learn to be open to new people, places, ideas and experiences. Develop confidence in your ability to entertain others. Do your best to maintain a lively curiosity and to continue developing your willingness to learn.

Plan a little fun every day; bring new things into your life; buy yourself something you will really enjoy; plan a brisk walk at sunrise; arrange to go somewhere —for a drive, to a movie or to dinner; visit new places, and don't be afraid to go alone. Let nothing be off-limits for lack of a companion!

PRACTICAL ASPECTS OF LIVING ALONE

8

Cooking for One

During my first year of living alone I did not believe that it was possible to cook a decent meal for one. I spent the first six months frequenting fast-food outlets. When I could no longer down another fast taco or hamburger, I survived on canned soup and TV dinners. Although this was a step up, the food was so bland that I began to lose interest in eating. I lost weight, caught frequent colds, and suffered all the agonies of an improper diet.

Nevertheless, perhaps because I was raised in a large family, I was stuck with the notion that cooking for one was a virtual impossibility. In my mind it simply could not be done, so I ignored the idea for quite a while. Other "loners" I knew were dining out regularly, and this reinforced my conviction.

By the end of that first year, however, my attitude began to change. One afternoon as I was working around my apartment, I was overcome by a craving for something *good* to eat. As I contemplated empty shelves and an empty refrigerator, I became angry and decided at that moment that I would attempt to master the art of cooking for one.

I made a list and went to the supermarket determined to stock my shelves and refrigerator with cooking supplies. I had fun on that shopping trip. As I acquainted myself with specialized sections of the supermarket, I realized that I did not have to buy in quantity. This allowed me to be a bit more creative in my selections and made the adventure a more personal one.

From the butcher I purchased specific items to build meals around: one pork chop, a quarter pound of bacon, and a T-bone steak. In the produce section I picked out a tomato, an apple, two bananas and a potato. Adding to a growing menu, I chose milk, some orange juice, cereal, and a carton of cottage cheese. My last purchase was a small German chocolate cake, my favorite dessert. At the checkout counter I realized delightedly that it would be mine to savor from the first bite to the last! Feeling proud and satisfied, I headed for home with a week's supply of groceries.

For some unknown reason that week is planted indelibly in my memory. I think it might be because I felt that I had made another significant stride along the road to living alone successfully. I will never forget the anticipation I felt prior to each cooking experience and the feeling of smug satisfaction once it was completed. It felt so good to be prepared to cook instead of wondering where the next meal was to be had. That feeling perpetuated itself and, as the years have gone by, I've come to enjoy cooking for myself in a way I never imagined was possible in the beginning.

PEG BRACKEN WAS RIGHT!

While I and other loners have mastered the art of cooking for ourselves and enjoy it, there are many more people for whom cooking an appealing meal for one is seen as more a chore than a pleasure. They will tell you that cooking and eating alone virtually prohibit them from living alone and liking it. These same individuals maintain, also, that dining out for every meal gets to be "old hat" very quickly. One fellow put it this way: "I wish they'd just invent a pill you could take at mealtimes."

Empty cupboards and refrigerators greet you where many singles reside. Some will tell you that they've never used their stoves. I know of one bachelor who removed his stove and refrigerator from his home altogether and converted his kitchen into a photography lab. He had resigned himself to eating in restaurants forever. The thought of learning to cook for himself was not only unappealing, but totally defeating.

Another bachelor complained frequently of being "forced" to dine out at every meal. He said he could see no sense in messing up his kitchen to fix a meal for just one person. He devoted much of his time to finding dining companions and locating untried restaurants.

A fellow near me has breakfast and lunch out and fixes himself bacon and eggs at home every night. He says it's the only thing he knows how to fix and that it simplifies his weekly marketing.

While it may sound as though I'm chastising men for doing a poor job of cooking for themselves, many women, who for the most part are better trained in the culinary arts than their male counterparts, do just as poorly. Though they may once have prepared elaborate meals for two or more, they seem literally incapable of putting a decent meal together for just themselves. All former cooking knowledge and skills seem to disappear. Worse yet, the desire to cook vanishes altogether.

Why is it that cooking for one and eating alone presents such a challenge? Why is nutrition often listed as the single largest problem facing those who live alone? Can anything be done to reverse this pattern?

To be fair, cooking for one isn't always easy. Most recipes are designed to serve four or more, and leftovers can be very uninspiring the third or fourth time around.

Boredom is another factor. When you are alone, mealtimes cease to be the events that they might be in a group or family setting. Many get the feeling that something has been lost in the transition.

A third factor is that *creative* cooking for one seems to many to be an impossibility.

On top of all this, some people just don't like to cook. If they happen to live alone and have no one to cook for them, they tend to turn to what is convenient—junk food, TV dinners, and the like.

Peg Bracken, author of the infamous *I Hate to Cook Book*, apparently anticipated that a substantial number of singles might fall into this category when she wrote the *Appendix to the I Hate to Cook Book* (Fawcett Crest Books, 1966) expressly for them. In fact, there *are* many single people, male and female alike, who hate all the fuss and bother attendant to meal preparation. "Where's the incentive?" they ask. "No one is going to reward me with rave reviews when I'm finished."

While I can identify and emphathize with this attitude, I am at the same time tempted to reply, "*You* can reward *yourself* with rave reviews and simultaneously contribute to your nutritional well-being."

Whatever your particular feelings on the subject are, consider the following: Eating is basic to survival. Since you have to eat to live, why not learn to cook some of your favorite foods? Even if you suffer from the "I-hate-to-cook" syndrome, try it anyway. Approach it aggressively. The more you work at it, the better you get. And the better you get, the easier it gets.

There are some simple things you can do to ease your way into learning to enjoy cooking and eating alone. While many nourishing single-serving entrees proliferate in the frozen-food market today, even more exciting is the opportunity to discover how to cook nourishing, interesting meals for yourself.

SPARTAN MEALS OR A GOURMET'S DELIGHT?

For the person living alone, meals and menus need not be elaborate. Some of the best may be the most simple. Cheese and crackers along with a fresh apple can make a nice meal. A quartered tomato filled with a tuna or cottage-cheese filling is an easy-to-prepare, good-to-eat choice.

I can testify from experience that it is possible to prepare a variety of well-balanced, first-rate meals for one with a minimum of fuss and bother. For efficiency-minded loners, simple, quick dinners might include such things as mini-stews or broiled fillet of fish with a fresh vegetable and a slice of warm sourdough bread. A cheese omelette served with applesauce and a toasted English muffin is another easily prepared, yet tasty treat.

Although I cook and dine in spartan fashion a good deal of the time, every now and then the "single gourmet" in me comes out and I'll prepare something fancy for myself—maybe Veal Picatta Uno or Mini-Teriyaki Meatloaf or Asparagus-Cheese Soufflé. In the early days of learning to cook for myself, I might have scoffed at the idea of preparing elaborate dishes for one, but not anymore. Everyone's cooking/dining routine needs an occasional lift. Concocting a gourmet's delight for yourself can be both a palate-pleasing and a mentally uplifting experience.

There are many single gourmets out there—people for whom cooking an interesting meal, if only for themselves, is one of life's chief delights. Since the kitchen is no longer strictly women's territory, many men are heading for the nearest range and are cooking up a storm. They are chopping, blending, slicing and sautéing like mad, secure in the knowledge that they are part of a growing trend.

Singles are flocking to cooking classes across the country—some learning to prepare gourmet cuisine—and not just because cooking is an enjoyable hobby. For many it is, or will be, a necessity. Others are looking to combat what they consider to be the "singles-cooking doldrums" with refreshing, easy recipes that look appealing and taste appetizing.

I've known many single individuals who have had a real commitment to fine cooking and fine eating. They pay special attention to those simple yet exquisite touches that can transform a mediocre dish into a splendid one. Working with unusual and delcious combinatons of flavors and ingredients, they help make cooking and eating alone more than just a function of refueling.

I've been fortunate over the years to have collected some easy recipes from these culinary wizards. And ease of preparation isn't the only attractive feature: most involve no waste, and some leave you with useful, tasty leftovers.

Selected Favorites from Single Friends

My neighbor Jack is a very meticulous, very organized man who channeled his love of mathematics and logic into a career as a computer programmer. He likes to spend his evenings tinkering in the kitchen as a way of relaxing after a day on the job. Simplicity is his culinary trademark, his recipes reflecting his work with basic formulas. I chose to begin with his burger recipe because it is both a good starter for the reluctant single chef and a welcome taste treat for the seasoned gourmand. Add a favorite salad, bread and beverage, and call it a great idea.

Jack's Perfect Hamburger

⅓ lb. ground beef
1 teaspoon cold water
¼ teaspoon Worchestershire sauce
salt and pepper

In a small bowl lightly mix beef, water, Worcestershire and pepper with a fork. Shape into patty using a light touch. Heat a small, heavy skillet; sprinkle with salt. When a drop of water sizzles in pan, add hamburger (If meat is very lean, you may have to add a pat of butter to pan.) Cook one minute over high heat to sear; reduce heat and cook one minute more. Turn patty; return heat to high and cook 1½ minutes or more, as you prefer.

For a different taste, remove patty and add two tablespoons of wine to pan; heat and stir to loosen brown bits. Pour over hamburger. If you like more flavor, toss meat with two teaspoons capers and one teaspoon minced onion. Still more flavor: omit capers and add one teaspoon prepared mustard to meat.

Angie is as competent in the kitchen as she is in her work as a legal secretary. She enjoys cooking for herself as well as for friends and is famous for the "special touches" which give her dishes distinction, appeal and extra good taste. Her recipe is ideal for those times when you feel like treating yourself royally. It also lends itself to entertaining in that it can easily be doubled or tripled for extra guests.

Angie's Elegant Steak

1 6-8 ounce beef tenderloin steak
½ tablespoon butter
¼ teaspoon salt
freshly ground pepper to taste
1 tablespoon dry red wine
1 tablespoon crumbled blue cheese

Pan-fry steak in butter three to four minutes on each side. Season with salt and pepper. Remove to heated platter. Stir red wine and blue cheese into pan juices. Cook until smooth and heated through. Spoon sauce over steak and serve.

The "perfect bachelor" (his description) is alive and well and producing screenplays in Southern California. Dave's busy schedule and irregular hours force him to eat out during much of the week, but the weekends permit him to use his creativity in the kitchen. Turning out wonderful brunches is his forte.

Dave's Nature Omelette

Omelettes can serve many delicious purposes in the life of a single person—breakfast, brunch, lunch, dinner or midnight snack. Try Dave's specialty any time of the day and see if you don't agree.

- 2 eggs
- 2 tablespoons water
- ¼ teaspoon salt
- 1 tablespoon butter
- 3 thin slices avocado
- 3 thin slices tomato
- ¼ cup alfalfa sprouts
- 2 tablespoons plain yogurt
- 1 tablespoon finely chopped walnuts

Mix eggs, water and salt; melt butter in omelette pan or skillet. Add egg mixture and cook slowly over low heat, pulling egg gently away from sides of pan to allow uncooked portion to fill the space. Just before folding, while top is still moist and creamy arrange sprouts, avocado and tomato slices on half of omelette. Fold in half and turn onto plate. Top omelette with yogurt and nuts and enjoy.

Busy professional people often have little time to shop and less time to cook. My friend Jeanne, however, employs the organizational skills required of her as an administrative assistant to compensate for the little time she has to devote to cooking—a favorite pastime.

Her secret is to keep a ready stock of basic ingredients and then to combine them in varied and interesting ways. The recipe which follows was chosen from her repertoire because it is a marvelously simple one made from ingredients which are common to many kitchens.

Jeanne's Fresh Fruit Salad with Creamy Dressing

You can't go wrong with this change-of-pace fruit salad. Its mild but exotic flavor complements almost anything you might care to serve with it.

- 1 banana, sliced
- 1 apple, halved, cored and sliced
- 1 large orange, cut into bite-sized pieces

Put cut fruit into serving bowl. In a blender combine the following ingredients:

- ½ cup cottage cheese
- ¼ cup orange juice
- 1½ teaspoons lemon juice
- 1 teaspoon honey
- ⅛ teaspoon salt

Pour blender mixture over the fresh fruit and toss. Allow to chill twenty minutes before serving.

Phil describes himself as a "perpetual student" who tired of cafeterias, coffee shops and fast foods long before he entered law school. He prides himself on his efficiency in the kitchen. Most of his creations are of the "meal-in-itself" genre. The following is patterned after a favorite casserole of his mother's.

Phil's One-Skillet Dinner

- ¼ lb. ground beef
- ½ tablespoon butter
- ½ cup medium noodles
- 4 ounces tomato sauce
- ¼ teaspoon salt
- dash pepper
- ¼ teaspoon basil
- ¼ cup grated Swiss cheese
- 2 tablespoons chopped parsley

In skillet, cook crumbled beef in butter until browned. Stir in uncooked noodles, tomato sauce, salt, basil and pepper. Cover and cook over low heat twenty minutes, or until noodles are tender, stirring occasionally. Sprinkle with cheese. Cover and heat two additional minutes, or until cheese has melted. Sprinkle with parsley.

College professor, life-long bachelor, lover of literature, bon vivant and kitchen chemist are a few of the terms that profile my friend Dan. When I asked him to share his favorite recipe, I was surprised that he offered something as basic as chili. According to Dan, his friends love to be invited to share this spicy dish. But Dan always thinks twice. He knows that chili is always better the second day. This recipe makes enough for you to enjoy it more than once.

Dan's Western Chili

- ¾ lb. ground beef
- 1 medium onion, diced
- 1 can pinto or kidney beans, drained
- 1 16-oz. can whole tomatoes
- 2 tablespoons chili powder
- 1½ teaspoons salt
- 1¼ teaspoon pepper

Brown the beef and onion at the same time. Add the can of tomatoes, breaking them up with your fingers. Stir in the chili powder, salt, pepper, and beans. Let simmer one hour.

Kay is a technical illustrator and "health-foods" advocate who spends most of her time away from her job playing tennis and dabbling in real estate. She says that she really does not like to cook but wants to eat well and therefore is willing to put in the necessary time in her kitchen.

I have enjoyed her marinated chicken on more than one occasion and asked for permission to reprint the recipe here because it is a one-meal entree which can also be enjoyed over several days. Kay advises you to choose your favorite pieces of chicken at the supermarket or butcher shop and try it. Couldn't be easier. Couldn't be tastier.

Kay's Marinated Baked Chicken

2 to 4 chicken pieces, skin and fat removed

In a large bowl combine:

2 tablespoons lemon juice
2 tablespoons soy sauce
1 teaspoon dry mustard
2 teaspoons salad oil

Add chicken and toss to coat. Refrigerate at least four hours, turning occasionally. Barbecue outdoors or place marinated chicken in foil-lined pan (for easy clean-up) and bake at 400° for forty-five minutes.

Although she had little time for cooking while earning her Ph.D., Sandy managed to maintain her reputation as a true gourmet. The epicurean delights which issue from her kitchen leave her friends talking for days. When she prepares lasagne, she makes the noodles from scratch. She uses nothing but fresh herbs snipped from the planter along her windowsill. Most of her recipes are prepared for company, have numerous ingredients and detailed instructions. I asked her for a simple rendering of a company favorite and she came up with the following. With a minimum of work and a couple of special touches, you'll have a mouth-watering, palate-pleasing delicacy that will leave you with a desire for more!

Sandy's Chicken Cordon Bleu

1 thin slice cooked ham, chopped
1 ounce Swiss cheese
⅛ teaspoon garlic powder
⅛ teaspoon pepper
⅛ teaspoon crushed thyme

½ chicken breast, boned and skinned
1 tablespoon flour
1 egg, beaten
2 tablespoon fine bread crumbs
2 teaspoons butter
2 teaspoons oil

Mix ham, cheese, garlic powder, pepper and thyme. Use to stuff chicken breast in pocket left by boning. Fold ends over to make roll. Roll chicken in flour, then in bread crumbs, coating well. In small skillet heat butter and oil; brown chicken on all sides. Place in a small, foil-lined baking pan and bake for twenty to twenty-five minutes in a preheated 375° oven. When done, chicken will feel firm to the touch. Serve with any pan juices.

Norma is a widow with a zest for living that is always infectious. It is impossible to be in her company and not become charged with her enthusiasm. She is a "no-holds-barred" lady for whom no place or experience is off limits. Dancing the night away at a nearby ballroom is common for her; backpacking in the Sierras or the Canadian wilderness is a frequent summertime activity.

Her contribution to this section came

as a result of a conversation we had about her approach to the holiday season. According to Norma, certain holiday celebrations or other special occasions just seem to call for turkey. But if you're cooking for one, what do you do? Thanks to the easy availability of turkey parts, you go ahead and have roast turkey.

A plump, meaty half-breast of turkey weighs just a little over two pounds, and this gives you plenty for dinner, with some left over for a wonderful turkey sandwich or two.

Norma's Roast Half-Breast of Turkey

1 2-lb. half-breast of turkey
½ cup 7-Up
salt, pepper and ground sage to taste

Sprinkle the inside of the rib cavity with sage, and the outside with salt and pepper. Bake in a foil-lined pan at 400° for fifty minutes to one hour, basting with 7-Up at thirty minutes and five minutes before serving.

These recipe selections are intended to spark your interest in cooking if you have lost it, or, perhaps, never had any to begin with. If you are a practicing chef it is hoped that you, also, will be motivated to try one or more of these specialties. For the true novice, more specific information is provided in the following section.

How and Where Do I Begin?

Organizing your supermarket shopping is a good place to start. If you are not particularly inclined toward cooking, cheeses, crackers, fresh fruit, canned soups and other simple items may comprise your shopping list. If you've been a victim of bare cupboards and a bare refrigerator, you will probably find it very nice to have these edibles on hand. From here you may even go on to expand your list as you make your trips to the supermarket. The idea here is to have things on hand from which you can put together a simple, nutritious meal.

A different approach, and one that may cause you to plunge headlong into cooking for yourself, is to select a favorite recipe from a magazine or cookbook, shop for the necessary ingredients, and then concoct your masterpiece. This may call for you to disregard quantity, but so what. Shopping for a particular recipe can provide real entertainment.

One friend of mine, who hadn't cooked anything more than boiled weiners in the two years since her husband had died, started anew with a recipe for beef stroganoff and ended up with not one, but several delicious meals. She said later that that one experience had changed her whole attitude toward cooking for herself. "I used to feel so limited by what I could fix for one person," she said, "but not anymore. I can fix anything I want to because quantity is never a problem. I use my freezer a lot, provide food for friends, and even feed my coworkers on occasion."

Plan by the week and shop by the week if you can. Buy in the smallest possible quantities when it comes to perishable items. Most grocers are happy to divide a carton of eggs in half. Butter can be purchased by the cube if need be. Many grocery items from soups to entrees are now available in single-size portions.

Make use of your freezer to store cheeses, breads, butter and other perishable foods. Some of the recipes I enjoy making serve six to eight people and cannot be reduced to a recipe-for-one formula. If I'm not planning to have company for dinner I simply freeze the leftovers in single-serving portions and make them part of another weekly menu plan.

If you're new to cooking and haven't done so, I urge you to purchase a good cookbook. Prior to the publication of cookbooks which specialize in recipes for one, I became an expert at halving—even quartering—recipes to accommodate my single-person appetite. Today, however, there are several good cookbooks with scaled-down recipes on the market. My personal favorite is Better Homes and Gardens' *Meals for One or Two.*

Besides being an excellent guide to small-scale cooking, with over 190 recipes for main and side dishes, desserts and beverages, it contains a "Tips and Techniques" section for planning and preparing meals. This section includes meal-planning guides, informatin on nutrition, food-buying hints, emergency substitutions, and special pointers on creating meals for one. Best of all, it is a cookbook for both beginning and experienced cooks, featuring tips for stocking and organizing your kitchen, selecting kitchen tools, purchasing basic cooking equipment and groceries, and storing food properly. Microwave cooking instructions are also included.

It is an excellent book to have on hand should you wish to invite a guest to dinner in that many of the recipes are designed to serve two. Conversely, many of the two-serving recipes are adaptable to a single serving.

Newspaper food editors have become highly cognizant of the fact that almost one-quarter of all U.S. households today are made up of one person. Instead of the rare recipes for one included in past weekly food sections, there now are many. I discover some good ones from time to time and collect them as a supplement to my cookbook favorites. A new recipe discovery can add a lot of "spice" to your weekly menu planning.

What Do I Cook It In?

The subject of necessary kitchen equipment and utensils enters here. I suppose that the only genuinely essential items in a kitchen are a knife, a spoon and a pan. Some who live alone have well-stocked kitchens already; others do not have so much as a pot. If you are devoid of cooking equipment, start somewhere. A good paring knife (for slicing fruits and cheeses, etc.) is an excellent first purchase. A set of pots and pans of various sizes is a wise buy, as is a set of mixing bowls and wooden spoons. Other useful paraphernalia might include a sturdy manual can opener, a serrated knife, a wire whisk, a peeler, a sifter, a spatula, a measuring cup and some measuring spoons, and a slotted spoon and ladle. And a set of single-serving freezer containers is a must.

This list is not meant to be comprehensive, but should serve to get you started. Every cook uses different utensils and appliances, and it will be up to you to decide what you need and make the necessary purchases as you go along. Do be aware that several manufacturers, apparently recognizing the growing market for small appliances among people who live alone, have produced such items as one-cup coffee makers and one-quart crockpots.

Wine by the Glass?

I never cease to be amazed these days at the growing number of products being marketed for the single consumer. Recently during my weekly sojourn at the supermarket something new caught my eye among the wine displays. The objects of my attention were petite decanters of wine topped by inverted wine glasses, attractively packaged and awaiting purchase by someone such as I. I chose a decanter of chablis.

This was not the first time I had left "skid marks" in a supermarket aisle. It had happened once before when I'd spotted cans of soup for one. I guess I am continually surprised and amused that, after being ignored for so long, the single consumer is now being considered a viable customer.

I thank the manufacturers of single-consumer items every time I use my one-cup coffee maker. For over ten years I'd been drinking instant coffee, because that was the only way I could prepare one cup at a time. Now I'm able to have the real thing—a single cup brewed from fresh-ground coffee. Commercialism aside, the taste and aroma are divine and were greatly longed for.

I have the feeling that the production of such items as wine by the glass, single servings of soup, mini-burger makers, etc., is only the beginning of an even greater catering to the single population on the part of the food and appliance industries. I anxiously await what's to come.

BE YOUR OWN GUEST AT A DINNER FOR ONE

Dining alone? Don't feel sorry for yourself. Think of the advantages. The dinner hour begins exactly when you want it to, not a minute sooner or later. You have the freedom to satisfy any particular craving or appetite whim in your meal planning and preparation. And you can afford to indulge yourself with a choice of entree that might seem extravagant if you had to multiply by two, four or more.

Cooking for yourself and eating alone can be fun, especially if you've given some thought to treating yourself as well as you should. Your menu planning and shopping can enhance your life alone considerably.

Just for the fun of it, try making a list of your favorite foods—all those mouth-watering delights you've enjoyed over the years. Then head out for the market intent on filling your cupboards and refrigerator with things you like to eat. Pamper yourself with the very best steak you can buy, a fine bottle of wine, a scrumptious pastry. Treat yourself to special foods. Seek out the local gourmet shop and see what strikes your fancy. When you are feeling bored or apathetic about cooking for yourself, the odds are good that some boxed or bottled delicacy will rekindle your interest.

Dining alone? Do it with style. Learn to cook the foods you love for yourself. You don't have to be serving someone or have someone serving you in order to make your meal an experience. Rather than taking the "what-difference-does-it-make-since-I'm-the-only-one-here" approach, try the reverse. Make every eating experience an enjoyable occasion:

—Combine foods as creatively as possible. Cook them with care and attention. Season them well with spices and herbs.

—Serve your meals attractively in pleasant surroundings. Set a table. Cut some fresh flowers. Put on some music.

—Establish a cozy place to dine and use it. Keep items of interest on hand—books, magazines, pictures, letters—things to occupy you while you leisurely dine.

—Make serving yourself fun. Reward yourself with rave reviews when you put together a culinary masterpiece.

I can almost guarantee that the more

creative and purposeful your menu planning, shopping and meal preparation are, the less painful dining alone will be. When I know that I'm going to be spending a Saturday evening alone, I will often plan to barbecue outdoors, weather permitting, or to fix an extra-special dish or dessert for myself. It gives me something to look forward to, keeps me constructively occupied, and gives me a tremendous feeling of satisfaction.

A widowed neighbor of mine spends each Saturday preparing elaborate casseroles. He says he likes having it to do and to look forward to, as well as being able to enjoy the finished product during the following week. Another friend has become a master of one-pot cookery. She's collected all sorts of crockery cookbooks, tries a new recipe every few days and invites friends in routinely to sample her results. (I remember when her weekly shopping list consisted only of the ingredients necessary to make bologna sandwiches.)

Cooking has become my personal form of therapy. Sometimes, when I'm feeling especially alone, I'll retreat to the kitchen, set to work on a chosen recipe, and before I know it I'm unaware of my aloneness and have something to show for the time spent. I find cooking an especially effective way to combat depression. Even if I only do something as simple as juicing a bag of oranges, I benefit in two ways: My mind is usually elevated because I am forced to redirect my thoughts, and I enjoy the fresh juice for days afterward. In fact, it makes me happy just to know it's sitting in the refrigerator waiting for me.

Cooking for one *can* be fun. Whether you are preparing a single dish or a casserole to be divided into single-serving portions, you can set the stage for any number of wonderful solo gastronomical experiences. Enjoying your meals alone *is* an integral part of living alone and liking it.

9

Living Locale

I have always said to people, "It's not *where* you live that's important, it's *how* you live." However, when I've discussed the subject with loners, I've made a point of stressing that where the person alone lives *is* just as important as how he lives.

There was a time when I would have stuck by my original premise and refuted the latter statement; however, a painful personal experience taught me otherwise.

THE CITY BY THE BAY

I'd been living alone for about ten years. During the first five I had occupied an apartment on a Southern California bay which I loved. There were many single people living in the area and we'd gradually melded into a little family of sorts. There was always someone on the beach to engage in conversation; canoeing, bicycling, dinner or movie partners were readily available. Everything a person could need was within easy walking distance—fine restaurants, a movie theater, a gourmet grocery, a well-stocked bookstore, shops of every kind, an ice cream parlor—even the great Pacific Ocean was only a few blocks away. It was a virtual loner's paradise.

On to Greener Pastures

Anyone who would leave such a place would have to be crazy. Looking back, I must have been. But the greener pastures of a beach town farther south beckoned with the promise of prosperity—both social and economic. I bade the bay apartment a sad and fond farewell and ventured to a large, plush apartment downshore.

The living was fine for the next couple of years. Then, one April, Uncle Sam got his teeth into this single taxpayer, and I was forced to look for living quarters that could provide me a sizable annual tax write-off. This was during the days when homeownership on the part of a single person was almost unheard of—and a virtual taboo. Shoving both aside, I defied convention, forged ahead, and found a cute little affordable house.

I suppose I should mention that although my income was stable and satisfactory, I almost didn't qualify for the loan because I was single. Ironic: The government was punishing me with an unreasonably high tax rate because I was single and was, at the same time, reluctant to allow me the opportunity to offset it.

I persevered, however, and after a time the place was mine. Pride of ownership took over immediately and within three years I had the place looking like a doll house. Working around the place and gradually adding things to the interior and exterior became a major source of entertainment for me.

I had marvelous neighbors, and friends dropped by frequently. All in all, it was a very satisfactory existence; I was happy there and Uncle Sam wasn't nipping at my heels.

Sometime during my fourth year there, however, I awoke to the realization that I had become a slave to the place. Mowing the lawn, gardening and pruning became nuisances rather than pleasures. The "greener pastures" had come to represent a 4,000-square-foot lawn which required weekly mowing; I had wearied of it. Added to that, my career was at a crossroads. It was time to move on. I put the place on the market and sold it a day later.

Solitary Confinement

I decided not to reinvest the profits from the sale of my house until I had made some career decisions, so I leased an isolated beach apartment in a resort town still farther south. I believed that I was so well adjusted to living alone by that time that the isolation wouldn't bother me. As it turned out, I almost died of it.

Except for the people at work, I had no regular human contact upon which I could depend—no neighbors to speak of—and friends felt my location was too far out of the way for other than occasional visits.

It was a year of almost literal solitary confinement and no less than sheer misery for me. Nothing seemed to work or have appeal. I even lost interest in my most treasured pastime—cooking. It was during this period that I began to be made aware of the importance of having access to other people in the vicinity of one's neighborhood. Of equal importance seemed to be the availability of ready sources of entertainment. I had to drive so far to get anywhere that I just didn't go. My once strong initiative toward outside social activity seemed to have deserted me.

I FIND MY NIRVANA

My career took a fortunately positive turn at this point and, after a great deal of reflection, I set out to find the "perfect dwelling place." Maybe it was an impossible quest, but I knew what I wanted and felt optimistic.

After a few months of searching I located a brand new condominium in a small all-adult complex. The unit itself was divine, the secure, wooded grounds were to be professionally maintained, and, to top it off, the complex was situated within a half-mile of a newly developed shopping and entertainment center. Too good to be true. I'd found my nirvana; I must have been living right.

Because I was the first resident to take occupancy, I was able to become acquainted with my neighbors as they moved in. I was not surprised to discover that half of them were single people also in search of a place where they could reside comfortably and have some of their social needs met at the same time.

Three years later we agree that it is the best of all possible worlds and the wisest move any of us has made. Good-neighborliness has created a feeling of family among the residents. While individual privacy is highly respected, caring and companionship are there for the giving and taking. This has contributed to the development of a strong, supportive social network within the complex. We enjoy one another's company at the pool, in the clubhouse, and in our homes.

At the same time, all kinds of opportunities abound right outside our gates—fabulous shopping and entertainment facilities, a well-maintained city park with jogging and walking paths, a popular nondenominational church, a junior college offering educational, cultural and recreational features—to name only a few. I find it to be the perfect total-living package for me as a person alone, and I feel very fortunate to have found it.

From these experiences and from discussions with loners, I have concluded that where the person alone chooses to reside has a significant bearing upon whether he will or will not enjoy solitary living. The choice of location is important primarily because of the implications it holds for social and recreational opportunities. Unless an individual is heavily inclined toward being hermit, I feel that it is wise to choose to live in a place which maximizes the opportunities for social contacts and experiences.

I have mentioned that mobility is one of

the advantages of the solitary lifestyle, and choosing a satisfactory dwelling place can be a worthwhile exercise of this option.

RELOCATION RAMIFICATIONS

Many loners find themselves in the position of considering a move from time to time. When the question of relocating comes up, it is wise to proceed cautiously, studying the choices and planning the move carefully.

When a partner—husband, wife or lover—leaves home, the person left behind may want nothing more than to move. The instinct is easy to understand and can perhaps be summed up in one word: *run!* The urge to change one's dwelling place is strong because there are reminders everywhere which can make the transition from being half of a couple to being a whole and single person all the more difficult.

For some, breaking and starting fresh can be a good idea. Sometimes it is a good thing to move. It can mean a break with the past and an opportunity to begin anew. Under the right conditions it can be beneficial. *However, no move should ever be made in haste.* Comfort and familiarity are especially important to a person alone. Leaving a familiar environment in a rush may cause one to feel exiled or isolated in his new location. Cutting through sentimental bonds is best done gradually. Saying a thoughtful goodbye to things which have meant a great deal to you can help to ensure a smoother and more lasting transition into your new life.

In relocating after death, divorce or separation, where do you go? Let's examine some of the more common options which are available to you.

Homeownership

The trend toward homeownership on the part of single people began in the early 1970's, and real estate professionals report that it is still growing. According to a major private mortgage insurance firm, the singles' apartment is slowly fading from the scene and is being replaced by a new status symbol: single homeownership.

For an increasing number of single people, the stability of homeownership is changing the essence of going it alone. Singles are leaving their apartments and buying homes, citing financial reasons as well as practical considerations. They are discovering that homeownership gives them a significant tax break, equity build-up, appreciation, and a hedge against inflation. They also cite other attractive features, such as neighborhood appeal, special privacy, a sense of "home," greater security, and the freedom to create a space tailored to their own tastes and needs.

I read with considerable interest a statement in a newspaper article which indicated that the emergence of the single homeowner has had an impact on establishing the single lifestyle as a desirable and acceptable one. How ironic, I thought. When I purchased my first home in 1970, not only, as I said, did I have trouble securing a mortgage because I was single, but I also was very reluctant to let anyone know of my decison. At that time there was a real stigma attached to being a single homeowner; it was easier to keep my secret than to have to explain that I wasn't relegating myself to spinsterhood or to permanent hermitage.

Homeownership involves making a commitment and gives you a chance to control your own financial security. It can also have the effect of centering your life around a more concrete (literally and figuratively) life structure. Besides that, it just feels good to invite people to *your* place. I've found, too, that apartment dwellers love to visit homeowners—most likely for that special feeling of being in an honest-to-goodness house.

Condominiums

Among many single-dwelling seekers there is a trend toward "multi-unit settings," usually condominiums or townhouses. Security, maintenance-free housing, built-in social advantages, and investment potential seem to be the most compelling motivators toward the condominium/townhouse option.

While the interior of a single unit can be decorated according to your particular taste, the responsibility for the exterior upkeep lies elsewhere. There are no lawns to mow, no gutters to clean, and no trash barrels to take out twice a week.

Usually condominiums are less expensive than single-family houses. Both houses and condominiums have continued to represent a good investment value for the person alone.

Adult Complexes and Retirement Communities

One day while having lunch at my favorite seafood restaurant, a spry lady of about seventy sat down beside me. We began conversing and suddenly she blurted, "I'm so glad to be able to talk to you. I've just done something very exciting and I love telling people about it."

She proceeded to tell me that her husband had died within the preceding year and that she had just moved into a place of her own in a senior citizens' community. "I'm living alone for the first time in my life, and I absolutely love it! I am enjoying my privacy and my freedom so much. In fact, I've never had so much fun. It's like starting life all over again!"

She confided that, when she was making plans to relocate alone to a town sixty miles from where she had always lived, many of her friends warned her that she was in for a dreadful time. "I made up my mind right then that I was going to make it a good experience no matter what. Adjusting was simply a matter of attitude. I love my new home and I'm making new friends every day. I haven't once longed for my former place."

Why would someone choose to leave a loved and familiar home and move into an adult complex or retirement community? Those elderly and not-so-elderly people alone who are opting for residences within such locations cite security, living near people of similar ages, the chance to make new friends, and more social and recreational opportunities as being the major advantages.

It doesn't take more than a look around for a person to realize that ours is a highly mobile society whose complexion has changed greatly over the last twenty-five years. Whereas in the past it was not uncommon for families to reside in proximate areas of the same *city*, they now live in areas scattered across the *country*. This can leave the person alone feeling abandoned. But in an adult complex or retirement community, people may not be so apt to feel left out. Many enjoy living in multi-unit settings where they can develop meaningful social contacts.

The composition of most neighborhoods changes over the years and these changes can create situations of social isolation for some people. Many have had the experience of awakening one morning to find themselves strangers in their own neighborhoods. In areas of common residence they have a chance to acquire a new sense of belonging and perhaps an opportunity for a fuller life.

The style of living in an adult complex or retirement community may not suit everyone. However, it is becoming an increasingly popular form of existence for many people in the over-forty age bracket. Of the numerous individuals I talked with who reside in common living locations, not one person found fault with his or her choice of living locale.

PUTTING DOWN ROOTS

Some loners, perhaps due to the nature of their condition, seem to live in a tentative fashion. They actively maintain a transient status, frequently moving from one place to another. Many seem to have no particular sense of belonging. For some this kind of "rootlessness" many contribute to feelings of anxiety, insecurity, discontent, and, in some cases, downright unhappiness.

A divorced gentleman revealed that a sense of not belonging anywhere nearly drove him crazy when he was first living by himself. "I had absolutely no sense of direction," he said. "I even tried putting down some roots in a few singles bars. However, it wasn't long before I realized that, for me, this was not the best way to form stable social relationships. It was then that I began to consider moving to a place that offered opportunities for well-established social contacts."

He chose an apartment in a complex famous for its low tenant-turnover rate. It wasn't long before he felt that he had acquired a feeling of belonging and his place of residence became an anchor of social stability.

It is important for people alone to establish homes for themselves—to settle down in a place they can call their own. While owning a place of their own may not be a top priority for many people alone, settling in a place they can call home is high on their list. These individuals claim that they benefit from a greater sense of stability and well-being.

Some who live alone, no doubt unwittingly in some cases, tend to slight themselves when it comes both to furbishing and to furnishing their living quarters. "Why should I do anything special just for me?" seems to reflect a common attitude. I'm sure you know my response by now: That's why you *should* do it. Because it's just for you.

Creating a warm, comfortable surrounding that nourishes and stimulates is a worthwhile endeavor for the person who lives alone, and it may also have a direct bearing upon whether he does or does not like solitary living.

It is very nice to have a place you enjoy coming home to, and, besides, adding the little special effects that make your dwelling place uniquely yours can be great fun. Taking time to create a cozy living environment will add meaning and significance to your life.

Where you live in relation to people, to outside entertainment and to other social opportunities may be a powerful factor in whether you are able to live alone and like it, and these things should be considered if you have the opportunity to choose your living locale. It is up to you to find the best place to meet your needs.

Some loners have been known to band together and form little communities of their own. They move into common areas, usually the same neighborhood or apartment building. These tightly knit groups form surrogate-family relationships and have built-in, supportive social networks.

For some loners it can be a freeing kind of thing to realize they can settle down anywhere. Others, however, may be forced by circumstance to live in a place not of their choosing. When such is the case, those affected need to work especially hard to find ways of meeting their living needs within their area of residence.

10

Your Own Money-Making Machine

The person alone has complete control over his financial destiny—if he chooses to exercise it.

This powerful concept is beginning to take root in the singles community at last. Single men and women in unprecedented numbers are investigating opportunities for investing in their financial futures. They are putting their money to work in a variety of ways in the hope of becoming financially secure. They seem to have become suddenly aware that the sooner they start stacking those financial building blocks, the better.

SINGLE PEOPLE AND MONEY MYTHS

For many years a certain negative mentality existed regarding finances and the single person. One aspect of that mentality held that the single person (especially the female) had no real purchasing power. Another mental stumbling block existed for individuals who, because they expected eventually to couple, tended to delay investing in their financial futures until they had acquired a partner. There were many singles living carefree existences, displaying an almost blatant disregard for the importance of building financial security for themselves.

Recently, however, the financial power of the single person, and of women in particular, has increased dramatically. Many states have enacted laws which prohibit discrimination against the single consumer. At the same time, many single individuals, men and women alike, are converting their earnings into worthwhile holdings—something that used to be almost exclusively the province of married couples and white-collar males.

A measure of the degree of interest in financial planning for singles was made evident to me not long ago on a Southern California campus offering a class on the subject. I arrived to register well ahead of the scheduled starting time only to find a standing-room-only situation.

One hundred and twenty people of all ages were crammed into a room designed to accommodate half that many. The rest were being turned away. Because I agreed to occupy a space on the floor in one of the aisles, I was permitted to stay. The instructor played to a packed house each week, while those who could not get in stood outside in the anteroom to hear what he had to say.

Why are singles today showing an unprecedented interest in their financial futures?

For one thing, there are more single people these days. For another, because many of them plan to stay single—or realize that they may—they are rapidly becoming aware of the value of building solid financial foundations for themselves. Other singles are finding it necessary to look into investment opportunities which can provide them some badly needed tax breaks.

Added to this is the all-important fact that *if you are alone, no one is going to undertake to ensure a sound financial future for you but you.*

SINGLE PEOPLE AND MONEY REALITIES

It comes as no surprise that there are more financially successful single men than women in our society. After all, pressure has never been placed on the ladies to succeed in the way it has been imposed on their male counterparts. Most of these well-heeled bachelors, following society's dictates, have set financial goals, gone out and hustled, and met their objectives. Perhaps some were motivated by the fact that they wanted to be well established in the event of marriage, but a good number were merely looking out for number one while fulfilling society's expectations.

Lest they get too confident, I would like to issue a warning to these fellows: Beware men, the ladies are close on your heels. Today, as never before, more and more women are independent and working and taking aggressive steps toward ensuring their own financial success. This is not to take away from the many long-time single women who have done well financially over the years but have gone relatively unnoticed in the context of the pre-women's liberation era.

There was a time when a majority of women acquired their holdings either through an inheritance or a divorce settlement. While this continues to take place, a far greater number are actively pursuing and achieving predetermined financial objectives. I know many single women who: own their own homes; own apartment complexes singularly or in league with other singles; have made prudent investments in the stock and commodities markets; have wide-ranging, well-rounded financial portfolios.

In the midst of all of the financially successful singles there exists a less fortunate group. Perhaps no one living on their own suffers more from a lack of financial knowledge than the widow or divorcée who has relied for years on her mate to manage the family finances. Some of these women have been long-time wage earners who, rather than manage a checking account of their own, have turned their paychecks over to the husbands. Some, of course, have never worked and are further disadvantaged.

Whether these women didn't bother to learn, or were never instructed in the basics of money management, they all wind up in the same boat, sailing toward financial oblivion. I will never forget the plight of a divorced friend who cashed all of her paychecks and paid her bills with money orders because she had the notion that balancing a checkbook was somehow beyond her capabilities.

Consider the comments of Marian H., a professional earning an excellent salary, who confessed to me that her life had been a "financial disaster" since her divorce: "Once the monetary controls were lifted, I lost direction and began to spend my money as fast as I earned it, with no thought for the future." She continued, "Being single somehow intensified my lack of financial planning. When there was someone else to provide structure, I was much better. I just plain have not wanted to accept the responsibility for my financial success. Also, I viewed my situation as temporary and, now, four years later, I am beginning to see that I need direction. In fact, I *want* it."

As our conversation progressed, her statements intensified: "I resent this part of being alone more than any other aspect. I am mad because no one is there to help me manage my money. However, now that I realize no one is going to come forward and do it for me, I am beginning to accept the fact that it is up to me to learn all I can and to set some goals for myself. I do not want to wind up a pauper."

People once a part of a couple often experience difficulty finding not only financial direction but financial balance as well. Take the case of Paul J., dovorced after a twenty-year marriage and earning a healthy five-figure salary: Paul came out of his marriage rejoicing in his financial freedom. When I ran into him shortly after the decree had been granted, he waved a wad of bills at me, saying excitedly, "Look at this! It's mine! All mine! And I can spend it any way I want to!"

After having been accustomed to the limitations of a family budget, Paul rebounded in the extreme, squandering away his cash like a kid in a candy store. It wasn't long before he realized that money spent in a random fashion didn't go very far and that he needed a plan for himself with funds committed to a meaningful purpose.

Several opportunities for acquiring basic financial knowledge exist for needy individuals — opportunities ranging from self-education to taking a class on the subject to hiring a financial advisor. Many singles are taking advantage of one or a combination of these in an attempt to better their understanding in an area critical to their success as a person alone. Unfortunately, however, there are still some laggers out there who continue to project an attitude of indifference.

"Why Should I Care?"

"Why should I worry about my financial future when I have only myself to be concerned about?"

To those who argue that they needn't worry about finances with only themselves to consider, I counter that they have given me the best possible reason to invest time and energy toward financial success—themselves. Since we carry the ultimate responsibility of providing for ourselves, it would seem wise to begin to assume and manage that responsibility as early as possible. Financial impotency is a condition to be avoided.

It has been said that you can get someone to discuss almost anything about himself—anything, that is, except his *money*: how much he makes and what he does with it. He may find it easy to make vague references to his financial situation, but don't get too specific, *please.* All of this serves to illustrate just what a personal issue money management is for most of us.

A definition of what constitutes financial success is an individual thing as well. It is therefore impractical to get into the area of prescribing specific success formulas. Some people prefer to invest their money in the stock market, some in real estate or long-term securities, others in gold or antiques —and these are but a few of the opportunities available to make your money grow.

While each investor could give you a logical reason for his or her choice, the point is that there are some very basic things *you* can do to get ahead financially *now* and to ensure your future solvency.

THE KEY TO FUTURE SOLVENCY

According to Ronald C. Gable, a certified financial planner in Southern California, ninety-five out of every one hundred people over the age of sixty-five suffer severely from financial mismanagement. They reach retirement with no savings at all. Only five per cent are able to stop working when they want to.

Makes you stop and think, doesn't it? Even with Social Security and a pension, the pleasures of your leisure time in retirement could be markedly diminished if you haven't developed a sound financial plan of your own.

Now Is the Time to Plan Your Financial Future

You may be twenty-five and spending your money on exotic vacations, or forty-five and making huge payments on a luxury automobile. Because you are single, you may have disregarded somewhat the idea of setting up a long-range financial plan for yourself.

Even though many singles are beginning to excel at managing their money effectively, there are others who have not yet taken steps toward developing any kind of personal financial plan for their lives. Aside from those who are renowned squanderers, those holding out or "postponing" for marriage may be the worst offenders.

The primary problem for them is that when a certain number of years elapse and no steps have been taken to convert their earnings into worthwhile holdings, those years and those earnings have been lost forever. The time to buy your house, for example, is *now*. If you should pair up next week, being a homeowner isn't going to hurt you.

No matter what your age, income, or

current living expenses, today is the time to start formulating a long-range financial plan. It is not as hard as you might think—especially if you know how to use your money wisely.

PLANNING YOUR FINANCIAL OBJECTIVES

To the uninitiated, the formulation of a financial plan may seem a difficult or unpleasant undertaking. Some associate it with extreme sacrifice; others fear it may involve complex financial calculations, which gives them reason to avoid it; almost everyone assumes that it will require a lot of tedious paperwork. However, financial planning really doesn't deserve all these negative connotations.

Setting up a financial plan is simply a matter of determining priorities and focusing on long-range needs and desires while, in some cases, foregoing a few momentary pleasures. It does require taking a realistic look at your financial picture, but rather than cramp your style, it should help create more money for the things which are truly important to you.

Personal financial planning, put very simply, is a way of helping you achieve your life goals. You have to figure out where you want to go and what you are willing to pay to get there before you can choose a means of getting there. The idea is to work up a plan that fits *your* needs and resources and which is designed to help you reach *your* goals. Determining what you will ultimately gain from better money management can be a strong motivating factor toward formulating your plan; it can also aid you in your goal-setting process.

The first step, then, is to *figure out what you want.* That can be more difficult than you may realize. You need to channel your thinking so as to compile a list of attainable wants, not a "wish list" of impossible dreams. For some that means getting help. If you cannot accomplish this on your own, you may wish to consult a personal financial advisor or a trusted friend.

One way to get a fix on your financial objectives is to sit down and do some extensive soul searching: What would you like to do with the rest of your life and how much are you willing to pay for it? You need to think about what you should do with your income.

When you get right down to it, there are really only two things you *can* do with it: spend it or save it. This often means making a choice between current enjoyment (spending it) versus future use of your earnings (saving it)—denying yourself now in order to get something you want later.

Working toward an easier, more pleasant future may be a goal. If you really want to own resort property and retire to it when you are fifty-five, then raising the capital to do that becomes your objective. If that can be achieved and you are willing to do the necessary sacrificing, the rest is pure methodology.

The ability to achieve the objectives you've set this way depends on your financial and emotional resources. *Determine and set realistic, practical goals for yourself.* Everyone knows that there are two quick ways to achieve your financial goals—by robbing a bank or by gaining an inheritance. Not many expect to do either, and so they must weigh all relevant factors and decide which objectives they can reasonably pursue.

Once you have accomplished this, you must move on to the second step, which is to *formulate a plan to achieve your goals.* Your plan, for example, may require the setting aside of a certain amount of your income each month for savings or investment. It may also involve a series of tradeoffs. You may have to give up certain things, at least temporarily, to pursue your long-range goals. This is as it should be, because it forces you to arrange your objectives in order of priority, which in turn helps you avoid wasting your time and efforts in the pursuit of insignificant goals.

The third and very vital step is to *set up a system to monitor and measure your progress.* This system can consist of anything from a simple household account ledger to complex graphs and charts depicting your long-range financial projections. Many people fail to get ahead because they neglect to keep track of where they are financially. What you need, in effect, is to structure a financial plan designed to let you know where you are so that you can track your progress toward your goals. It is imperative that you keep your system simple and well organized. This will help you avoid the common mistake of getting so lost in the labyrinth of personal money management that you lose sight of what you are attempting to achieve.

You must then *get into the habit of thinking and acting logically rather than impulsively*—of deciding rationally rather than rationalizing decisions—where money is concerned. This will help you avoid the common conflict of emotions versus intellect and steer you away from spending money foolishly or unnecessarily—money that can serve you more meaningfully by being incorporated into your overall financial plan. It may be an overstatement to say that all of our financial decisions should be made in the context of how they will affect us the rest of our lives; however, it is difficult to deny that such a consideration is strong reinforcement for making sound, rational judgments.

Make a concerted effort always to *use your resources effectively and efficiently.* This simply involves determining what you need to do to reach your goals, given your resources, and then finding the right way to do it. For example, if you have $2,000 you wish to invest, you need to find the investment that will give you the best return. Efficiency may well be the key to financial success.

Finally, make sure *that your financial plan is custom-designed for you.* You can't depend on succeeding financially the way someone else has. If you are working with a personal financial advisor, be sure that his or her recommendations are tailored to your needs and interests. Too many advisors would rather try to make you fit their plans. Perhaps the best advice is to be sure that your personal financial portfolio shows what you have bought—not what you have been sold.

Some final words of caution. As you construct and analyze your financial plan, bear in mind that a sound, well-developed plan will allow you to meet your current living expenses satisfactorily, to continue to build a solid reserve, and to create opportunities to make your money grow. A good plan should give you a feeling of security in knowing that you are covering all of your financial bases—living realistically in the present and planning for the immediate as well as the distant future.

ENSURING YOUR FINANCIAL SUCCESS

"The individual needs to view himself as a money-making machine. He is his own business."

When these statements were made to me by a young, single attorney, they quickly bored their way into my consciousness. Not only did they represent an aggressive approach to investing in one's financial future, but they reflected an attitude and philosophy that I felt were especially well suited to people alone.

Despite opinions to the contrary, it is not difficult to comprehend and apply sound financial principles to your life—to get *your* money-making machine going. You don't have to be in the six-figure income category to need financial know-how, either. The person earning $15,000 a year can benefit just as much proportionately if he understands and applies sound money-management principles.

It is imperative that the person alone learn as much as he possibly can about money management and that he utilize this knowledge toward building a solid foundation for financial success.

Accepting total responsibility for your financial success as a person alone is no small thing, to be sure. Fortunately, there are some significant things you can do to help ensure progress within your financial plan. We are all familiar with the age-old expression, "It's the little things that count." Well, this is no less true when it comes to getting ahead financially.

You can draw up the most beautiful plan in the world and yet undermine the whole thing in small, subtle ways that, while they seem to have no immediate effects, often manifest themselves in a cumulative explosion otherwise known as the "bottom dropping out." Or you may fall victim to the "negative-gain" syndrome—never really getting ahead due to the little ways in which you continue to defeat yourself financially.

What it amounts to in many cases is just plain old financial irresponsibility. There are, however, ways to assure solvency with a minimum of effort and a maximum of good common sense.

Becoming Your Own Economics Expert

So as not to frighten the unwary, the term "economics expert" as used here has a rather loose connotation, implying only that you be aware of and apply fundamental economic principles in the context of managing your finances. Being your own economics expert often involves nothing more than listening and observing carefully—listening to what people are saying whenever the subject of money management or finances is discussed.

Whether in a formal lecture or in casual conversation, what you hear may not have meaning for you at that point in time, or ever, but chances are good that if you store the information in your memory bank, you may be able to draw on it to your advantage at a later date.

Read business and financial news carefully. Use common sense to figure out what the data mean, applying the information when you can to your own money-management scheme. Let's assume, for instance, that you are interested in purchasing a foreign car and that you become aware that import tariffs on said car will be increased by a few hundred dollars at a specified time. The smart move is to buy the car you want prior to that time and save the extra money. The point is that if you give *no* preliminary thought to such a purchase, you may wind up paying a much higher price than necessary.

Newspapers and magazines can be excellent sources of current financial information. Bookstore shelves are stocked with texts devoted to money mangement, covering everything from the most basic to the most complex. In these economically turbulent times it pays more than ever to be financially well read and there are some outstanding contemporary works available:

Harry Browne's *New Profits from the Monetary Crisis;* Douglas R. Casey's *Crisis Investing: Opportunities and Profits in the Coming Great Depression;* Howard Ruff's *How to Prosper During the Coming Bad Years.* The point, of course, is for you to learn as much as you can by reading material which is applicable to your particular situation.

Observe what is going on in the financial world. This may entail nothing more than knowing what a neighbor's house has sold for so that you know the approximate value of your own house, or being aware of the least expensive loan you can get should you need to borrow money. It is not that difficult to acquire control and confidence in managing your assets. With a minimum of effort and know-how, you can learn how to compute your net worth, how to work out your cash flow, how to make the most of your assets, how to make major money decisions wisely and how to plan effectively for the future.

Learn as much as you can. The more you know, the more your money-management situation will reflect it and the less likely you will be to fall prey to financial ignorance or to be taken advantage of financially.

Given the choice we would all opt for freedom from worry about money. For most of us, however, there is never enough. It becomes a matter of hanging on to what we have and managing it wisely.

Sound money management becomes, in effect, a behavioral science. It can be learned. A great deal of self-discipline goes into it—mostly the self-discipline to think long term and to remember that every financial decision you make is done in the context of supporting you for the rest of your life.

Money may not be the purveyor of happiness, but buying freedom from financial worry can certainly add to life's pleasures. Eliminating financial pressures from your life as a person alone can add immeasurably to your capacity for living alone and liking it!

Get your money-making machine going and keep it functioning smoothly and efficiently at all times. Most important, be aware that you probably are not going to succeed financially if you neglect your "machine" or if you turn its operation over to someone else.

11

On Your Own

Perhaps when you began reading this book you were dubious not only about the note of optimism expressed in the title, *Living Alone and Liking It,* but about the implicit promise as well. Perhaps you questioned your capacity for finding value in the single lifestyle—even doubted your ability to survive on your own.

Now that you have made your way through the preceding chapters, it is hoped that your perspective has been altered positively, that you will be able to adjust, to find value in the lifestyle—that you will learn to live alone and like it.

If you let it, living alone can be joyful. It can be a time of curious exploration, of individual and personal fulfillment, of unlimited freedom, of new experiences, and, most promising, a time of a growing perception of yourself.

Living on your own puts you in complete charge of your life, vesting you with total responsibility for yourself. This responsibility should be considered a blessing rather than a burden, for it can mean so many positive things:

—Living alone can make you a more capable and whole human being. It is an experience which enables you to work with the various pieces of your "self" and put them together in an honest form. The ability to do this without external interference or reliance on another greatly enhances your potential for personal growth.

—As a result of such growth, the person who lives alone is able to reach out and relate to others in a deeper, more vital way. Because there is a lesser tendency to take human relationships for granted, they take on greater significance and become more gratifying.

—In living alone, by confronting the life tasks of changing, developing, building and growing alone, by moving toward significant personal accomplishments on your own, and by assuming the responsibility for determining your own destiny, you develop true integrity.

—Living alone gives you a chance to develop a trust and belief in yourself, to expand your horizons by taking risks occasionally and by experimenting with life, to experience the confidence that comes of self-reliance. Some people go through life believing in the competence of others—

never in their own. In living alone you discover that your capacities are real. It is a fantastic feeling!

—Living alone lets you make your own decisions without having to give into or compromise with someone else. Some of us never get to try out our decision-making abilities until we are, in fact, on our own. When we find ourselves doing a good job of being our own companions, critics and counselors, it just plain feels good!

—Living alone gives you the opportunity to experience the joys of being free, allowing for a wide variety of experiences. You are able to engage in a type of ongoing goal setting and pursuance that may not be open to you in a more restricted lifestyle.

—Mastering single living can provide you with a type of personal depth and strength unlike any other experience in that it requires you to draw upon all your resources in order to do a good job, to make it a profitable, worthwhile experience. It can cause you to realize dimensions of yourself you never knew existed— dimensions which, when discovered, can lead you to make the ultimate statement about yourself as a person alone:

"I am capable."

LOOKING TO YOURSELF

At times we are all guilty of looking outside ourselves, mostly to other people, for things to "fill us up"—to make us feel "whole" or "complete." But to depend on others for such things as our happiness or our security is putting a lot of responsibility on them when, in fact, the responsibility rests with us.

A young divorcée made a significant observation following a rather difficult adjustment to living alone: "I've made an important discovery during my first year," she said, "and it is simply that *I* am the only one who can make me happy. I used to believe that it was up to my husband to make me happy; I now know that another person can add to my happiness, but only I can make myself happy."

Looking to yourself, being able to depend on yourself, is what being on your own is all about.

Sharing vs. Experiencing Alone

You are the only person in the world who has your particular thoughts and feelings. Another person can be made aware of them through conversation or shared experience, but no other person can truly absorb them. That we ultimately exist only unto ourselves is, I think, an indisputable concept and one which, when acknowledged, makes for a better acceptance of our "on-our-own" status.

The fact is, experiences are never truly shared; they can't be. Two people may be present at the same event, but each will take away a unique perception of it, a unique feeling about it. If you accept this type of logic, you understand that it simply is impossible to be "one with another"—not to be "alone" according to pure definition.

Given that everything, in the final analysis, is experienced alone, the question becomes, "Can the presence of another person actually affect my perception of the experience?" This is not meant to discount the feelings of pleasure you may derive from another's company, but merely to point out that it is only company and that what is perceived by each is purely singular in nature.

Because we live in a couple-oriented society, some people regard themselves as incomplete human beings until they have paired up; indeed, these people often attempt to complete their identities by "coupling." The fact is, however, that "identity" is not something one can acquire from another person. To attempt to do so is to risk becoming a fraud—an amalgam of parts which can never comprise a "complete" individual.

What it boils down to is that you are on your own in life no matter what your circumstances. If you can acknowledge and accept your essential aloneness, you can then see your options more clearly and see living alone as an expansion of possibilities that opens doors, not closes them. In other words, if you are "alone" or "on your own" anyway, why allow the desire to couple or the concept of pairing to represent a major stumbling block on the road to living happily and successfully on your own?

LIVING ALONE AND LIKING IT

The key to a successful life alone lies in your attitude toward it. How you feel about it and the manner in which you approach it are the two most important factors. If you look upon it as a potentially negative experience, it will be. If, however, you pursue it as an adventure which has room for pleasure and growth, it will provide both.

As a first-time experience, living alone can be difficult; but learning to live alone can, in the transition, be good for you in that you have an opportunity to grow while adapting to the change in lifestyle. It can also be fundamentally good for you if you question whether you possess the resources to survive on your own. It is a self-affirming experience to discover that the answer is *yes*!

Living alone offers you the opportunity to assume full authority over yourself, giving you in turn the power to take charge of your life. It is up to you to do so in constructive, self-determined ways—to take responsibility for your own health, wealth and happiness, to make your own connections with the world—in essence, to find meaning for your life.

There are as many ways of finding a happy, rewarding life alone as there are people with the courage to seek them. Your experiences will vary from those of others, depending on your age, economic status, whether you are single, separated, divorced or widowed, and whether you have children. What one person may regard as awful or disastrous, someone else may take in stride. It's all relative to the person, to his or her personality and particular situation.

In living alone successfully you develop a formula for living that will serve you inestimably the rest of your life. Your ambition should be to make a whole, contented life for yourself *now*—to avoid living as if you were suspended or, worse, immobile—and to arrive at a place where you can enjoy a totally fulfilling existence on your own.

We have so little time for the truly important things in our lives that we should want to spend it in the most personally profitable and enjoyable ways possible. Whatever you do, don't sell yourself short. You *can* learn to be your own inspiration and to have a good time wherever you are, whether or not anyone else is with you. You *can* function well as a totally independent person. You *can* create and sustain a well-balanced social life. You *can* discover and nurture interests which are of special significance to you. You *can* be your own source of strength, comfort and encouragement. You *can* give yourself good counsel. You *can* meet the challenge of creating a full, rich, interesting and satisfying life *on your own!*